CBASIC™
USER GUIDE

Adam Osborne
Gordon Eubanks Jr.
Martin McNiff

OSBORNE/McGraw-Hill
Berkeley, California

CBASIC is a registered trademark of Compiler Systems, Inc.

Published by
OSBORNE/McGraw-Hill
630 Bancroft Way
Berkeley, California 94710
U.S.A.

For information on translations and book distributors outside of the
U.S.A., please write OSBORNE/McGraw-Hill at the above address.

CBASIC USER GUIDE

 234567890 DODO 898765432
ISBN 0-931988-61-6

Cover design by Mark Miyashiro.

Acknowledgements

The authors gratefully acknowledge the programming contributions of Wendy James.

Contents

1
Beginning With CBASIC

CBASIC FIRST BECAME available to the microcomputer industry in 1977. Other versions of the BASIC computer language were already on sale, usable on many microcomputer systems; what was so special about this one? Actually, very little distinguished CBASIC from the others until late 1978, when CBASIC Version 2 was released. This new version was just what many small software firms had been looking for: a programming language suitable for business computing, with many capabilities not found in other versions of BASIC. These firms started developing programs for mass distribution; accounting programs, financial and statistical packages, even complex file management systems were written in CBASIC.

You probably have CBASIC programs already working on your computer. Thousands of other people do. Because CBASIC works with the widely adopted CP/M operating system, programs will run on many different makes of microcomputer. Why is this important? Computer programs are being sold, much like records, through retail outlets. You certainly would want to buy a record which was playable on almost any turntable, and the same principle applies to computer programs. Other reasons for CBASIC's popularity will be covered later in this chapter.

Two Buzzwords You Must Understand

Two computer buzzwords came up in the first two paragraphs of this book: *programming language* and *operating system*. A programming language is a restricted set of words and symbols which represent procedures, calculations, decisions and other operations a computer can carry out.

Computers use binary logic to carry out every operation they perform. It is inefficient to program a computer using binary logic, since that would mean generating a sequence of ones and zeros. Programming languages were invented so that programs could be understood by people, yet be automatically reducible to the binary instructions which a computer needs to carry out its assigned tasks.

An operating system is a collection of programs that work as a supervisor for the computer. When you turn on the power for your computer, the operating system is always the first program to run. With some machines the operating system will automatically load into the computer's memory. With others, you have to press a RESET button or go through some short procedure that starts the operating system. While the computer itself is an aggregation of chips, circuit boards and connected boxes, it is the operating system programs that give this aggregation the operating characteristics of a computer system.

CBASIC — HOW IT WORKS AND WHAT IT DOES

CBASIC computer programs exist in two forms: the program you write and the program you run on the computer. You write a CBASIC program using a *text editor.* A text editor, or word processor, is yet another program, which receives information typed on the computer keyboard and stores the information on a diskette. Text editors will store a CBASIC program, a memo, or the chapter of a book. (Incidentally, this book was written using a text editor.) With descriptive words such as PRINT, INPUT, DATA, and others, you create the text of a program in the CBASIC language. This text is called the *source program.* CBASIC will convert the source program by *compiling* it into a highly condensed series of symbols which the computer can execute. This set of symbols is called the *object program.*

CBASIC comes in two parts: the compiler, which reduces the text of a source program to machine-readable symbols of an object program, and the *interpreter,* which (as its name implies) interprets the symbols of the object program and thus executes the program. CBASIC is unique among BASIC languages because it contains both a compiler and an interpreter. Other languages will compile a program into *machine language,* which is the sequence of binary instructions we discussed earlier. Some versions of BASIC are called *real-time interpreters;* they allow you to enter the program and run it in one operation. Real-time interpreters let you interrupt a program and go through it step-by-step to spot and remedy errors. Machine language compilers have the advantage of speed; that is, the program compiled into machine language will execute faster because the program has been converted to the computer's "native tongue," and interpretation is not necessary. Real-time interpreters have the advantage of eliminating compilation and tracing a program while you run it, but they can be quite slow. This tracing feature is only helpful to the programmer interested in fixing program errors, so when you use an interpreter BASIC, you pay a price in speed every time you run the program.

You may be wondering why CBASIC compiles *and then interprets* a program. At first you might think this wasteful. Actually, CBASIC conserves memory almost as well as a compiler, plus having features not available on most compilers. It does not have features that other BASIC interpreters have, but it is faster than they are. In this world of trade-offs, CBASIC is no exception. Its biggest advantage is known mostly to programmers: CBASIC allows *structured programming*. Structured programming makes error-free programs a possibility. People can read and write structured programs more easily. If they make better sense to a programmer, they will no doubt make better sense to a machine.

Errors in Programs

Errors are bound to happen. Even if you are a good programmer, you will have many. If you are a bad programmer, you will probably not anticipate them or even be able to fix them when they occur. Programmers daunted by errors have wondered, at one time or another, if their computer is out to get them. Errors occur in complex programs and simple programs. They occur both obviously and insidiously, rarely when you expect them.

CBASIC recognizes two kinds of errors: *compiler errors* and *run-time errors*. Compiler errors are misuses of the computer language itself; e.g, misspelling PRINT (a CBASIC "verb") as PFINT. These mistakes are relatively minor and cause little frustration, because as a programmer's language abilities improve, these errors decrease in number and severity. They are also quite easy to fix.

If you finally compile a CBASIC program which has no compiler errors, you can run the program on the computer and see if it works in practice. Run-time errors occur when CBASIC cannot do what your program specifies. The reasons for this vary, and actual causes of errors are not always easily detectable. Solving run-time errors is a painstaking step-by-step process. This book will attempt to teach you understanding of the language as well as its usage; this will keep the errors in your programs to a tolerable level. Once you start using CBASIC extensively, you can turn to Appendix A of this book for complete descriptions of CBASIC errors and how to correct them when they come up.

Your Computer System

CBASIC will work with your computer system if you have CP/M, MP/M, CP/NET, or other operating systems which imitate CP/M. Ideally, your computer should

Photo by Harvey Schwartz

Figure 1-1. A Computer System

have two or more disk drives, a CRT terminal, and a printer. CBASIC recognizes all of this equipment, but first you will have to make some distinctions which make learning easier.

Figure 1-1 illustrates the various components of a typical business computer. In computer parlance, these are *physical devices,* that is, the computer's paraphernalia. These physical devices are treated as *logical devices* by CP/M. To illustrate the difference, consider how you can use a stereo system. You have perhaps a cassette recorder/player and a turntable, along with a tuner/receiver. You can variously select sound input sources: tape, radio, or turntable. You can also select sound output devices: headphones, speakers, or, if you want to store the sound you get through the receiver, you can select the cassette recorder as the sound output device and then listen back to it.

In this case, we have two logical devices: sound input and sound output. By selecting where input comes from and output goes to, the physical devices are all linked together in a logical framework; that is, although you may have many physical devices attached to your sound system, you will usually need one logical device for sound input and one logical device for sound output. It is the same with computers, with the difference that computers deal with data, received from and sent to various physical devices.

When you write a CBASIC program, you will need to concern yourself with three logical devices: the console device, the printer, and the diskette drives. The console device (normally a CRT terminal) is used for data entry from the keyboard. Either the console or the printer can be used to display or print information. The diskette drives (as many as four on your system) are used for data input and data output. These are the logical devices you work with when programming. Of course, your own common sense will tell you which device to use, once you become more proficient at programming.

FIRST SESSION: EDITING A CBASIC PROGRAM

Although you may have a fully featured text editor program on your computer, CP/M has its own text editor, called ED. ED is primitive. It lacks conveniences normally found in expensive text editors. A tortuous narrative about every available program of this kind is not the concern of this book. If you are not using ED, make sure that you understand the operation of your text editor. On the assumption that everyone who uses a CP/M system also has ED, let us move on to the first session.

Assuming that the ED program is stored on the diskette in drive A, the first entry is ED followed by a file name and a carriage return:

```
A>ED FIRST.BAS
```

The entry above will *create* a file on the diskette in drive A. This means that CP/M will reserve space on the diskette to contain the text you are about to enter. This space is a diskette file, and the letters appearing after ED represent the name of the file. If you create a file that you later want to change, you will use ED to alter it. In the case of this file, FIRST.BAS, ED responds by displaying:

```
NEW FILE
*
```

which means that CP/M will create the file on its *directory*. The directory is a reserved portion of the disk which contains the name, size, and location of every file on each diskette. This message does not appear for files which you have already created.

Entering New Text

Next, an asterisk (*) appears at the beginning of the next line, indicating that ED is ready to use. This character is a *prompt;* its function is to notify you that ED is waiting for instructions. To start typing the program in, you have to enter a *command character,* a one-letter code which ED responds to. The first command character is I, which stands for Insert. After entering this character and pressing the RETURN key, the prompt character disappears and you can begin typing in text:

```
*I
PRINT "FIRST PROGRAM"
```

If you aren't familiar with ED, try entering the text shown above. This illustration is an extremely simple CBASIC program. Once you have entered the text, you have to signal ED that you want to leave insert mode. Do this by pressing the Z key while holding down the CTRL key (Control-Z). The prompt will reappear:

```
* ◄——— Control-Z pressed
```

Now at this point, go over the text entered so far and check it for errors. To look at all of the text from the beginning of the file, enter the following set of command characters:

```
*B#T ◄─────── Enter command characters
PRINT "FIRST PROGRAM"
*
```

If you enter this set of characters and press the RETURN key, all of the text you entered will display. The first letter, B, instructs ED to point to the beginning of the text. ED maintains a *character pointer;* this pointer is a number which ranges in value from 0 to the number of characters in the text file, and it literally points to any one of the characters in the file. The B command simply sets the pointer to 1, which represents the beginning of the file.

The next two letters, #T, instruct ED to type out each line of text in the file, until the end of the file is reached (#represents the end of the file, and T stands for "type"). Check each line of text against the illustrated text above. If there are any discrepancies, you will have to change the text; otherwise, when you try to compile this program CBASIC will notify you of compiler errors due to misspelling.

Fixing Typographical Errors

If you find an error in the entered text, you can fix it by reentering the entire line, or by substituting the erroneous letters. If the word PRINT were misspelled as PRNIT, you could use ED to switch the letters back to their correct order. The following set of commands:

```
PRNIT "FIRST PROGRAM"
*SNI^ZIN^Z
*
```

changes the word PRNIT to PRINT. The first character, S, is a command character which stands for Substitute. The S command instructs ED to search through all of the text for characters matching those immediately after the S. After S, notice the two letters NI. These are the letters to change. After these two letters, notice ^ Z. This is actually one character entered on the keyboard, not two as it might imply. ^ Z means that the operator entered Control-Z; this signifies the end of the set of characters to search for. After ^ Z, the letters IN appear. This is the set of characters to replace the first set (NI) with. In other words, you are directing ED to:

1. Search text for the characters NI.
2. Replace the NI with IN.

In its English form, the SNI ^ ZIN ^ Z means "substitute the first two characters 'NI' you find in the text with 'IN'." Substitutions move the character pointer up to the character immediately after the last character substituted. Therefore, the character pointer would symbolically move as follows.

P	R	N	I	T		"	F	I	R	S	T		P	R	O	G	R	A	M	"
1	2	3	4	5	6	7	8	9	10	11	12	13	14	15	16	17	18	19	20	21

Pointer at the beginning of text

P	R	N	I	T		"	F	I	R	S	T		P	R	O	G	R	A	M	"
1	2	3	4	5	6	7	8	9	10	11	12	13	14	15	16	17	18	19	20	21

Pointer located at the text to substitute

P	R	I	N	T		"	F	I	R	S	T		P	R	O	G	R	A	M	"
1	2	3	4	5	6	7	8	9	10	11	12	13	14	15	16	17	18	19	20	21

Pointer after substitution

If you just made a substitution and you find that you have to make another one nearer to the beginning of the text, enter the B command. This will reset the character pointer to the beginning of the text.

Saving the Program on Disk and Using CBASIC

To indicate that there are no changes needed for the text you entered, enter the E command character, which stands for End. This command writes the text onto the diskette, saving it in the file FIRST.BAS. You could have chosen any name for the file, but its last four characters, .BAS, have to be the same for every CBASIC program you write. Enter the E command as shown:

```
*E

A>
```

This saves the text on the diskette, signals to ED that you are finished editing the file, and returns you to CP/M. The next step is to compile the program.

To compile a CBASIC program, enter:

```
A>CBAS2 FIRST
```

Assuming that the CBASIC compiler and interpreter programs CBAS2 and CRUN2 are on the diskette in drive A, this will compile your program. Entering CRUN2 notifies the operating system, CP/M, that you want to run the CBASIC compiler. FIRST is the name of the text file which contains the CBASIC program;

notice that the last four letters of the file name, .BAS, can be omitted because CBASIC automatically adds these last four letters. Of course, using FIRST.BAS would do no harm.

When your program compiles, you will see it displayed line by line, as shown below:

```
CBASIC COMPILER VER 2.07
    1: PRINT "FIRST PROGRAM"
    2: END
NO ERRORS DETECTED
CONSTANT AREA:        8
CODE SIZE:           19
DATA STMT AREA:       0
VARIABLE AREA:        0
```

This is called the *compiler listing.* If this program had any compiler errors, you would see them displayed along with the program. The information printed at the end of the compiler listing are called *compiler statistics;* these indicate the size of certain areas of memory which your CBASIC program will use when you run it. Later, you will see how to use these compiler statistics in more involved programming exercises.

Now run the program by typing:

```
A>CRUN2 FIRST

CRUN VER 2.07
FIRST PROGRAM

A>
```

Entering CRUN2 directs CP/M to execute the CBASIC interpreter and run the program named FIRST. When you used the CBASIC compiler it created a new file, named after FIRST.BAS. The last four characters of the new file are .INT. This file contains the program in its highly condensed, executable form, and these four characters are added after FIRST when you run the CBASIC interpreter. If you entered CRUN2 FIRST.BAS, you would get an error. The interpreter cannot understand source programs, only compiled programs.

The program is supposed to display FIRST PROGRAM. After doing this, the program ends and returns control of the computer to CP/M. You have just edited, compiled and run your first CBASIC program. Some of you may be excited; others may be less impressed by the results from so much initial work. Expect to be underwhelmed every so often when you write programs. Details quickly pale in significance once you realize what results you can get as you become more proficient.

2
Data Types

COMPUTER PROGRAMS WORK with many types of information; we refer to this information collectively as *data*. Data can consist of numbers or words. We call numbers *numeric data*. Words are called *text data,* or *strings*.

Consider a company's payroll ledger which lists employee names, social security numbers and net pay as follows:

JOHN B. DOE   123-45-6789   512.34

"John B. Doe" is a group of words which a computer can treat as a single text data item. Obviously 512.34 qualifies as a numeric data item, but what about social security number 123-45-6789? Is it numeric, or is it text? The two dash characters (-) are classified by a computer as text data; therefore, the entire social security number must be treated as a string. Although the word "string" is a computer buzzword (presumably derived from text being a string of characters), it is used so frequently to describe text data that we should start using this terminology as soon as possible.

Thus the employee information shown above consists of the following three data items:

NUMERIC DATA

All numbers are numeric data items; there are, however, two types of numeric data which CBASIC recognizes: *integers* and *floating point numbers.*

Integers

An integer is a whole number, without any decimal point and fractional component. CBASIC recognizes integers with values ranging between +32767 and −32768. Here are some examples of valid and invalid CBASIC integers:

-27	Valid
2	Valid
2.5	Invalid because of the decimal point and fractional part
2.0	Valid because it is equivalent to 2
60000	Invalid because it is too large
-30000	Valid

Floating Point Numbers

Floating point numbers (also referred to as real numbers) can have integer or non-integer values. Every valid integer is also a valid real number, so why bother separating integers and real numbers in different classes? The answer is that integers occupy less memory space. CBASIC stores four integer numbers in the same amount of memory occupied by one real number.

CBASIC stores real numbers with a precision of 14 decimal digits. But this 14-digit limit does not affect the magnitude of numbers which can be represented; it only affects numeric accuracy. Here are some examples:

1234567890	A 10 digit number
1234567890.1234	A 14 digit number
123456789012340000	An 18 digit number with 14 digits of precision

To understand the significance of 14-digit precision, think of money. If money amounts must be accurate to the penny, then 14 digits allows up to one trillion dollars to be accurate to a single penny. But from one trillion dollars to ten trillion dollars, accuracy will be to the nearest ten cents. From ten trillion dollars to one hundred trillion dollars, accuracy will be to the nearest dollar. Unless you are using CBASIC to program the federal budget, the 14-digit precision limit will prove adequate.

When calculating with real numbers, CBASIC *rounds* numbers longer than 14 digits. When CBASIC rounds a number, the least significant digits past the 15th decimal place are dropped. The 14th digit increases by 1 if the 15th digit is .5 or higher. Once CBASIC rounds the real number to 14 decimal places, it drops the 15th digit altogether. Here are some rounding examples:

1234567890.1234567	becomes	1234567890.1235
1234567890.1234321	becomes	1234567890.1234
1234567890123456.7	becomes	123456789012350
1234567890123432.12	becomes	123456789012340

Exponential Notation

Floating point (real) numbers can be represented using the simple decimal point format shown above, or you can use exponential notation. Exponential notation represents numbers as follows:

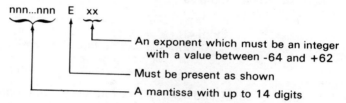

Here are some examples of real numbers and their exponential notation equivalents:

Number	Exponential form	nnnnn	xx
11.02	1.102E1	1.102	1
110.2	1.102E2	1.102	2
0.001102	1.102E-3	1.102	-3
100000	1E5	1	5
0.0000547	5.47E-5	5.47	-5

The maximum and minimum possible values for real numbers in CBASIC are:

Largest number: 9.9999999999999E62
Smallest number: 1.0 E-64

Binary and Hexadecimal Notation

You can represent integer numeric data in binary (base 2) or hexadecimal (base 16) format as well as the familiar decimal format. As a beginner you will never need to use these numeric formats; as your skills advance, you will find these alternate numeric notations very useful. The theory behind the material in this section is covered in *An Introduction to Microcomputers: Volume 0, The Beginner's Book,* from Osborne/McGraw-Hill.

Binary numbers are represented as a series of digits which can only be ones or zeros, ending with the letter B for "binary." Here are some examples:

10110B   is equivalent to 22 decimal
1001010B   is equivalent to 74 decimal
100110101B   is equivalent to 309 decimal

Hexadecimal notation introduces six new digits beyond the decimal system; A, B, C, D, E and F (which correspond to decimal values 10 through 15). In CBASIC you can use hexadecimal notation for integer numeric data. All hexadecimal numbers must start with a base 10 digit; that is, to represent FF hexadecimal, you must place a zero at the beginning of the number; in other words, express the quantity as OFF. Always place a zero digit at the beginning of a hexadecimal number if the first digit is A, B, C, D, E, or F. To denote to CBASIC that the number is in hexadecimal notation, you must place the character H at the end of the number. Here are some examples:

1FH   is equivalent to 31 decimal
2FAH   is equivalent to 762 decimal
OFAH   is equivalent to 250 decimal
FAH   will be interpreted as a
         three character text string

Note that binary and hexadecimal formats are *not* separate data types; they are special forms of expressing integer numeric data in CBASIC.

STRING DATA

CBASIC requires that string data be enclosed in quotation marks (" character). Any character other than a single quotation mark can be part of a string. If you want a quotation mark to appear in the string, two consecutive quotation marks must be used. A single string data item can be up to 255 characters long.

Here are examples of string data items:

"2584 Milliken Causeway"
"Please re-enter data"
"Acct #3035-22-124AT"
""""No Comment"""", said the politician."

This final example generates the string:

"No Comment", said the politician.

CONSTANTS AND VARIABLES

Data can be either *constant* or *variable.* If you wanted to find the circumference of a circle of any radius, you would use the general formula:

$$circumference = 3.14159 \times 2r$$

The number 3.14159 is the value *pi.* It is a constant value, necessary to calculate the circumference of any circle. The radius of the circle, *r,* is the variable in the formula; its value can change, yielding a different result. You can represent any type of data in a CBASIC program as constant or variable.

Consider the "formula" needed to compute payroll, and the employee net pay amount. Rather than describing net pay using a constant dollar amount in the program, we could instead use a variable for this amount and write a general formula for payroll calculations, substituting new values into the formula for each employee in the company. In order to calculate the formula, CBASIC needs names for each variable. To illustrate the concept of a variable name, let us assign the name NETPAY to a variable representing employee net pay. We can demonstrate the way variables work using the following CBASIC statements:

```
LET NETPAY = 512.34
PRINT NETPAY
```

The first statement assigns the value 512.34 to the variable named NETPAY. The second statement prints the value assigned to NETPAY. In this instance the value 512.34 prints. At some other point in the program, NETPAY can be set to a different value. You need do nothing special to create variables within a CBASIC program; whenever a new variable name appears, CBASIC incorporates the variable into your program.

About Variable Names

As described earlier in this chapter, there are three types of data:

1. Strings (also called text data)
2. Integer numeric data
3. Real (or floating point) numeric data

Variable names can be from 1 to 31 characters long. The first character of a variable identifier must be a letter of the alphabet. The rest of the name can be letters, numbers or periods (.). Special characters (such as &, !, @,*) are not allowed. If a variable name has more than 31 characters, the excess characters are ignored when CBASIC compiles your program.

The last chararacter of every variable name specifies the type of data which the variable holds. When you write a CBASIC program, you have to name each variable. Make sure that the type of data you use matches up with the type implied by the last character of the variable name. Variable names for strings must end with a dollar-sign ($) character; so at least two characters, an alphabetic first character and a terminating $, must be used in order for it to be identified by CBASIC as a variable which will only hold text data.

Here are some examples:

```
NAME$
N$
XYZ$
EMPLOYEE.NAME$
NAME.AND.ADDRESS$
A1234X$
```

CBASIC identifies integer numeric variables with a percent character (%) as the last character of the variable name. Therefore integer numeric variable names, like string variable names, must contain at least two characters. Here are some examples of integer numeric variable names:

```
NO%
NO.%
PQRS%
I%
INDEX.VALUE.25%
```

If a variable name does not end with a dollar character ($) or a percent character (%), CBASIC assumes the data type to be a real number. Here are some examples:

```
NUMBER
NO
VARIABLE123
NAME.AND.NUMBER
X25
```

There are a few important properties of variables which you should keep in mind at all times.

Certain variable names are not allowed in CBASIC; they can cause errors in your program because the compiler does not interpret them as variable names. You may mistakenly use a variable name which also functions as a *key word* in CBASIC. Variable names that cannot be used by the programmer are called key words. Appendix C lists the CBASIC key words. As long as your variable names are not identical to any key words in the table, your programs will compile and run properly.

CBASIC treats variable names with different type endings as different variables. For example, CBASIC treats AX, AX$, and AX% as three separate and distinct variables, unrelated to each other. In practice you should try to make CBASIC variable names descriptive and unique; it will help you understand the programs you write.

ASSIGNING VALUES TO VARIABLES

Until a value has been assigned to a variable, it will have zero value if it is numeric, and a null or "empty" value if it is a string. Of course, programs should always assign integer values to integer variables, real numbers to real variables, and strings to string variables. If you try to assign data of one type to a variable of another type, this is a *mixed-mode* assignment. Sometimes CBASIC will resolve mixed-mode assignments; other times it will not, causing a program to end abnormally, or *crash*.

Assigning an integer constant to a real numeric variable is acceptable, because integers are also valid real numbers. If you assign a real number to an integer variable, and the real number is within the range of possible CBASIC integers (between −32767 and 32768), CBASIC will drop the decimal portion (if any) of the real number and properly assign the real number to the integer variable. The real number's decimal portion is dropped without rounding; this dropping of the decimal portion is called *truncation*. If the truncated real number is not a valid integer, CBASIC will assign an unpredictable integer value to the variable. Here are some examples of real numbers being assigned to integer variables:

123.765	becomes 123
123.12	becomes 123
1.999	becomes 1
4732968.4	generates an unknown, erroneous value

If you attempt to assign a string constant to an integer or a real numeric variable, CBASIC will display an error message. If you assign an integer or real number to a string variable, then the number is accepted as a numeric string. In other words, the numeric digits are treated as characters rather than components of a number.

ARRAYS

A company will not use a computer to process its payroll if it only has a few employees. Payroll programs handle hundreds of employees; even though each employee's exact pay data (rate, filing status, etc.) is different, every employee's record contains the same type of information. CBASIC allows you to organize masses of similar data in lists called *arrays*.

Must a program use a separate and unique variable name for each employee name, each social security number, and each net pay amount?

NAME1$	SSNO1$	NETPAY1
NAME2$	SSNO2$	NETPAY2
NAME3$	SSNO3$	NETPAY3
NAME4$	SSNO4$	NETPAY4
etc.	etc.	etc.

It would make no sense to use variable names as illustrated above. You can use a single variable name to represent a large number of equivalent data items. These variables are called *array variables*. In contrast to the previous example, we could use an array variable for all of the employee names and another representing all of the employees' social security numbers. A third numeric array variable name represents net pay for each and every employee. Although only one variable name is used to describe a list of items, array variables have a *subscript* in parentheses, just after the variable name. The subscript points to a specific employee name in the array of many employee names. This may be illustrated as follows:

NAME$(I%)   SSNO$(I%)   NETPAY(I%)

The subscript is an integer illustrated above by the variable I%. The subscript points to a specific "line" in the list of employee names. Consider the following list of data items:

JOHN B. DOE	123-45-6789	512.34
ALICE J. PARKS	473-62-8217	697.74
JACK A. WRIGHT	489-49-2718	484.37
PETER B. BLACK	921-38-7217	363.63
etc.	etc.	etc.

Array elements would be assigned values as follows:

NAME$(1)	=	JOHN B. DOE
SSNO$(1)	=	123-45-6789
NETPAY(1)	=	512.34
NAME$(2)	=	ALICE J. PARKS
SSNO$(2)	=	473-62-8217
NETPAY(2)	=	697.74
NAME$(3)	=	JACK A. WRIGHT
SSNO$(3)	=	489-49-2718
NETPAY(3)	=	484.37

An array variable can have more than one subscript. For example, we could create the following single variable, with two subscripts to identify employee names and social security numbers:

NAMESSNO$(I%,J%)

This "two-dimensional" array variable would be assigned values as follows:

NAMESSNO\$(1,1)	=	JOHN B. DOE
NAMESSNO\$(1,2)	=	123-45-6789
NAMESSNO\$(2,1)	=	ALICE B. PARKS
NAMESSNO\$(2,2)	=	473-62-8217
NAMESSNO\$(3,1)	=	JACK A. WRIGHT

etc.

Subscripts for a two-dimensional array are analogous to grid coordinates on a map, with one subscript pointing to the vertical coordinate and the other subscript pointing to the horizontal coordinate. You can expand arrays to more than two dimensions. Try to visualize three subscripts now: the first pointing to a page in a booklet, the second pointing to a particular line on the page, and the third pointing to each word on the line. By using a three-dimensional string array called BOOK\$, it is possible to "get" the third word on the 25th line of page six:

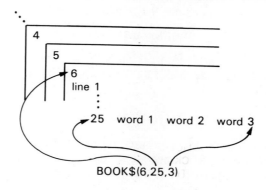

Syntax for Array Variables

As mentioned before, array variables do the job of grouping masses of similar data together under one generic name. The data so grouped must be the same in type; i.e., within a single array you cannot mix integer and real numbers, string and numeric data, etc. Subscripts for array variables are valid CBASIC integers, used either directly with constants or indirectly via variables. You could even use another array variable to identify a subscript. Here are four array variable subscript expressions; they are equivalent to each other:

NAME\$(3)
NAME\$(I%) if I% is equal to 3
NAME\$(I%(J%)) if I%(J%) is assigned the number 3

If you specify a real numeric value instead of an integer for a subscript, then CBASIC will convert the real numeric value to its integer equivalent. The CBASIC program will execute more slowly, but otherwise no harm is done. If you specify a real subscript with a value outside that of valid CBASIC integers, the program may access an incorrect element of the array.

The DIM Statement

In order to use array variables in a CBASIC program, you have to *declare* the array variable name and the size of the array itself. The DIM statement declares array variables. DIM stands for "dimension."

Before using an array variable in a program, you must declare it to CBASIC using the DIM statement. The DIM statement also declares an array's largest subscript value, thus allowing CBASIC to set aside data storage in the computer for the array. Consider the following simple example:

    DIM NAME$(100)

The DIM statement illustrated above assigns 101 elements to the NAME$(I%) array. If you want NAME$(I%) to have just 100 elements, you could dimension it as follows:

    DIM NAME$(99)

CBASIC considers zero as the first subscript in an array; some programmers find that using a 0 subscript is a confusing source of programming errors. It is far easier to visualize NAME$(1) as representing the first element in a list, rather than the second. It is therefore common practice to ignore the initial 0 subscript value. For example, even though the statement

    DIM NAME$(100)

allows NAME$(I%) to have 101 values, you could elect to use 1 through 100 only. NAME$(0) goes unused, wasting a small amount of memory space.

When the array is first declared in a DIM statement, every element has a null value if it is a string, or a 0 value if it is numeric. Here are two more examples of DIM statements:

    DIM NAME$(100), SSNO$(100), NETPAY(100)

NAME$(I%), SSNO(I%), and NETPAY(I%) each have 101 elements. But the dimensions shown suggest that subscript values ranging between 1 and 100 will be used in each case, with the 0 subscript being ignored — not by CBASIC, but by you the programmer.

    DIM NAMESSNO$(100,2), NETPAY(100)

NAMESSNO$(I%,J%) has two subscripts; the first can have values ranging from 0 through 100, the second can have values of 0,1, or 2. In this case you pay a high price in wasted memory space if you ignore all 0 subscripts: you will waste 104 storage spaces. All 101 values of the first subscript are wasted while the second subscript is 0, and all three second subscript values are wasted while the first subscript is 0.

Although DIM statements do not have to appear at the beginning of a program, they should appear in one prominent place — preferably at the beginning! This again is a matter of style which you may not fully appreciate until you have to go searching for a DIM statement buried somewhere in a large program.

You can use a constant *or* a variable to declare the highest subscript for an array. In this case, the current value assigned to the variable is used as the highest subscript value. This may be illustrated as follows:

```
I% = 100
DIM NAME$(I%), SSNO$(I%), NETPAY(I%)
```

Here is another example in which a dimensioned integer variable is used to specify a subscript:

```
DIM I%(2)
I%(1) = 100
I%(2) = 2
DIM NAMESSNO$(I%(1)), I%(2)), NETPAY(I%(1))
```

A name that is used to describe a non-subscripted variable can be re-used to describe a subscripted variable. CBASIC treats the two as separate and distinct variables. Here are some examples:

```
A% and A%(I%) are different variables
A%(I%) and A%(I%, J%) are conflicting
                       representations of
                       the same variable
A$, A%, A$(X%), A%(X%),A and A(X%) are all different
                                       variables
```

Certainly CBASIC allows you tremendous flexibility in naming variables. However, errors can persist in programs you write if you name simple variables and array variables so similarly.

3
CBASIC Program Organization

If You Are An Experienced Basic Programmer, Chapters 14 and 15 probably tell you all you need to know about CBASIC. But if you are a beginning programmer, do not read these chapters first; they present too much information with too little explanation. You should learn CBASIC by reading the chapters of this book in order. When you encounter a new statement and do not understand how it is being used, then refer to Chapter 15 for a description of the new statement.

MODULAR PROGRAMMING

The first and most important step when learning to program is to understand good practices. Nothing could be more detrimental to your long-term programming aspirations than arbitrarily stringing together a list of BASIC statements which happen to make a computer perform your desired task, and calling it a program. Programs must have structure and organization. There are two reasons for this. First, your programs will be easy to understand if you organize them well. Second, they will be easier to modify or expand in the future.

If you have some simple task that you want a computer to perform, perhaps it can be defined using one small program; but even as you are writing this small program, bear in mind the possibility that someday you may want to include it in a larger program. When you are writing larger programs which perform more complex tasks, the best approach is to design each task in its smallest parts, call each part a *module* and then write each module separately. Not only will this make your program easier to follow, it will also make your next program easier to write. Why? Because you can use today's modules in tomorrow's programs.

FLOWCHARTING

The most direct way of organizing a computer program before you write it is to draw a *flowchart*. A flowchart is a series of symbols which depict the operation of a program, often called the flow of control of the program. In Table 3-1 are shown the various symbols that may be used in flowcharts. You will see two kinds of flowcharts. A *system flowchart* is an overall block diagram which shows how the modules of a program interact as a whole. Look at Figure 3-1, which shows a simplified system flowchart for a bank's automated teller machine.

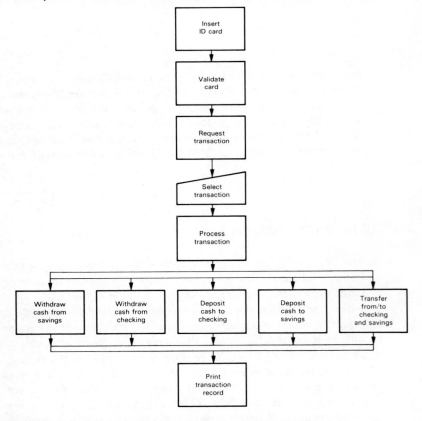

Figure 3-1. System Flowchart for a Simple Automated Teller

Table 3-1. Flowchart Symbols Key

Symbol	Description	Symbol	Description
Arrow	Designates direction of program flow.	**User Instructions**	The operator must perform a duty outside of progam.
User Input	Keyboard entry.	**Process, Note**	Describes a program action, or may contain a note to the user.
Display	Describes or quotes what is displayed on CRT screen. Quotes are shown in bold type, all capitals.	**Terminal**	Designates program start, program end, or return to main program.
Disk Action	Describes an action taking place on disk drive; do not interrupt program during this process.		
Decision Yes No	Direction of program flow determined by a "yes" or "no" answer to the enclosed question.	**Connector** or	Continue program at matching code (note direction of arrow). Connector circles in regular weight are incoming connectors (flow transfers TO the connector). Connector circles in bold weight are outgoing connectors (flow transfers FROM the connector).
Printout	Report printed by printer on standard paper.		

Every box indicates a module in the program, each of which depicts a general operation. All system flowcharts should be written this way, because they give an overview of how the program works. Compare the system flowchart with that shown in Figure 3-2. This is called a *program flowchart* because it documents each decision, calculation and operation of the "validate card" module shown in the system flowchart.

Is a flowchart always necessary? In practice, most programmers do not use them; that is one reason why computer programs have errors in them, some of which are detected years after the programs were written. Imagine trying to build a house without blueprints, fixing construction mistakes as they come up. What kind of home do you think you would wind up with when you finished? Always commit to paper what you cannot keep straight in your head.

CBASIC has features which let you use programs as modules in larger programs; these are called *library features,* and are explained in detail in Chapter 8.

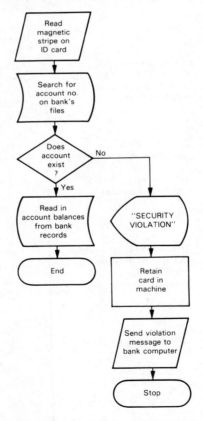

Figure 3-2. "Validate Card" Module — Program Flowchart

PROGRAM STRUCTURE

It is a good idea to structure every module and program you write before you begin to flowchart. Divide each task into phases; you may find when you look at a module that it needs breaking up into even smaller modules. These are the most common phases:

1. *Data definition.* Assign constant values and specify what variables the program will use.
2. *Data input.* Get information, either from the operator or from peripheral devices, which the program will operate on.
3. *Data processing.* Perform operations on data.
4. *Data output.* Print and/or display results of data processing phase.
5. *Data update.* Store results of data processing phase on disk, tape or other machine-readable medium.

By using a consistent structure you will find that programs are easier to use and less prone to error.

CBASIC STATEMENT FORMAT

Every CBASIC statement contains one or more *key words* which describe calculations, decisions, input or output. Key words are listed in Appendix C. Numbers, variable names and special symbols appear in some CBASIC statements; these are called the *parameters* of the statement.

You may use upper-case or lower-case letters in CBASIC statements. The CBASIC compiler automatically converts lower-case letters to their upper-case equivalents, unless you specifically suppress this conversion (using a feature called the *toggle switch,* described in Chapter 16). Wherever one blank space is allowed in a CBASIC statement, you can insert as many blank spaces as you wish. This allows you to write more legible programs. By indenting CBASIC statements as you would in an outline, you can generate programs that are easier to read.

You can spread a single CBASIC statement across more than one line; conversely, more than one CBASIC statement may occur on a single line. Use a backslash character (\) to continue a CBASIC statement on the next line. For example, the statement:

```
IF NUMBER = 0 THEN GOTO 100
```

can be expanded with backslashes as follows:

```
IF NUMBER = 0 \
   THEN GOTO 100
```

The two program statements are equivalent in CBASIC. You can put text after the \ character, and CBASIC will ignore this text. In the statement below, we take advantage of this feature by putting an explanatory remark after the backslash:

IF NUMBER = 0 \ CHECK FOR END OF PROGRAM
   THEN GOTO 100

A \ character cannot appear in the middle of a variable name or key word. Therefore the following statement would generate an error:

IF NUMBER = 0 TH \
   EN GOTO 100

When you want to put more than one statement on a single line, use a colon (:) to separate one statement from the next. This may be illustrated as follows:

NUMBER = 0:GOTO 100

There are some exceptions to the rules given above. These exceptions are defined in Chapter 15, and discussed where appropriate in other chapters.

LINE NUMBERS

Most versions of BASIC require that every program statement have a line number. Line numbers must be integers, and each line number must be greater than the one preceding it. Line numbers are optional in CBASIC, and are necessary only if the line number is referenced by a statement elsewhere in the CBASIC program. CBASIC line numbers do not have to be in any order, nor do they have to be integers. A line number may be any real or integer number. Line numbers may include a decimal point and fractional component, or they may be represented using exponential notation. Exponential and real line numbers are treated as different numbers, even if they have the same numeric value.
Here are some examples of valid CBASIC line numbers:

100
23.456 ⎫
2.3456E1 ⎬ These are interpreted as different line numbers
40000
147700000

The only rule is that a CBASIC line number must have 31 characters or fewer.

THE REMARK STATEMENT

In order to make programs readable, you will want to include comments that explain what is going on. You can add comments to CBASIC programs in one of two ways:

1. You can write comments beyond a \ character on any line, or
2. You can use a remark statement.

Anything appearing on a line after the key word REMARK is ignored by CBASIC. You can shorten the key word to REM if you like. This is the only CBASIC key word which you can abbreviate. Below is a short program that uses remarks to describe what the program is doing. You will probably have little trouble understanding the program, even if you have never seen the statements used before.

```
      REM Keep a running total of numbers less than\
          or equal to 100 in integer variable LESS%.
          LESS%=0
      REM Input the next number.
  100     INPUT NUMBER
      REM Add 1 to MORE% if NUMBER is greater than 100.\
          Otherwise, increment LESS%.
          IF NUMBER > 100 THEN MORE% = ·MORE% + 1\
                          ELSE LESS% = LESS% + 1
      REM Go back to line 100 for another entry.
          GOTO 100
          END
```

A REM statement can share a line with other statements, or it can be the only statement on a line. If a REM statement shares a line with other statements, then the remark must be the last statement on the line. A colon can, but does not have to precede a remark statement on a multi-statement line. Here are some variations of lines taken from the short program illustrated earlier, showing different valid uses of the remark statement:

```
      MORE% = 0: REM Initialize the counter
      LESS% = 0  REM Clear this counter also
      IF NUMBER >0 THEN MORE% = MORE% +1 \ Increment MORE%
                   ELSE LESS% = LESS% +1 REM or LESS%
```

The following line uses a remark incorrectly because another statement follows it on the same line. CBASIC will ignore the statement following the remark, treating it as if it were part of the remark:

```
      MORE% = 0:REM Initialize the Counter: LESS% = 0
```

You can use a backslash character to continue remarks across two or more lines:

```
REM     * * * * * * * * * * * * * *  \
        *  PRIMES.BAS     11/30/81  *  \
        * = = = = = = = = = = = = = =  *  \
        *  THIS PROGRAM GENERATES  *  \
        *        PRIME NUMBERS        *  \

        * * * * * * * * * * * * * * *
```

THE STOP AND END STATEMENTS

Every program should end with a STOP statement or an END statement. This is not a CBASIC rule, but it is good programming practice. A STOP statement causes program execution to cease in an orderly manner, closing any disk files which may be open at the time. An END statement tells the CBASIC compiler that the end of the program has been reached. If your program has no END statement, the CBASIC compiler places an END statement after the last statement in the program automatically. Any text in a CBASIC program which comes after the END statement will be ignored by the compiler.

4
Simple Data Input and Output

DATA INPUT AND OUTPUT MODULES are frequently the largest and most difficult parts of a program to write and test. These modules communicate with human operators; because the computer is a productivity tool, it is especially important to write programs which operators find easy to use. We are going to approach input/output programming as a series of steps, beginning in this chapter with CBASIC statements that receive data input from the computer's terminal keyboard and display results on a CRT screen. We will illustrate step-by-step procedures to write, enter, compile and run a CBASIC program. The step-by-step illustrations use the CP/M editor, ED, which we discussed in Chapter 1. If you have a CP/M compatible word-processing system, you can certainly use it to enter your CBASIC programs.

THE INPUT STATEMENT

The INPUT statement is used to receive data from the keyboard. The INPUT statement allows you to display a message on the console device before the operator enters data from the keyboard. This message is called a *prompt*. The prompt is a string constant enclosed in quotes and followed by a semicolon. It is not always necessary (or desirable) to have a prompt with an INPUT statement; CBASIC allows you to use INPUT statements without displaying a prompt to the operator. An INPUT statement can receive any number of data items from the keyboard.

The following examples illustrate the various forms of the INPUT statement and its parameters:

REM Display no prompt; get one real number; assign its value to N.
INPUT N

REM Display prompt; get one real number; assign its value to N.
INPUT "Enter a number:"; N

REM Display prompt; get two real numbers;
REM Assign the values to M and N, respectively.
INPUT "Enter two numbers:"; M, N

REM Display prompt; get a real number, integer and a string
REM from the keyboard. Assign these to A, A%, and A$.
INPUT "Enter a number, an integer, and a string:"; A, A%, A$.

THE PRINT STATEMENT

When you want your program to print or display data, use the PRINT statement. Unless specifically instructed to do otherwise (by the LPRINTER statement), the output goes to the display.

The PRINT statement is identified by the key word "PRINT," followed by one or more items to be output. The items can be real, integer or string variables or constants. When you PRINT a variable, the latest value assigned to it prints. If you want to PRINT a series of variables and constants, all mixed together on the same line, separate each item with either a semicolon or comma. These punctuation characters have special meaning to CBASIC; if you use a semicolon, there will be one blank space after each real or integer data item printed, and there will be no spaces after string data items. If you use a comma, however, CBASIC will go to its next tab stop after printing either a numeric or string quantity. Tab stops occur every 20th print position on the printer or display. The comma is useful if you want to print data in a table format.

Here are some examples preceded by explanatory remarks:

REM   Print the number 123.4
PRINT 123.4

Here is the display:

123.4

column 1

REM   Print the two numbers 123.4 and 567.8
PRINT 123.4, 567.8

Here is the display:

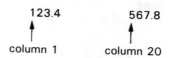

Here is the same PRINT statement with a semicolon separating the two numbers:

PRINT   123.4;567.8

Here is the display:

In order to illustrate the INPUT and PRINT statements, we will create the following short program:

```
10 INPUT "ENTER A NUMBER:";N
20 PRINT "THE NUMBER IS:";N
30 GOTO 10
40 END
```

Note the next-to-last statement. GOTO causes the program to go back and execute statement 10 repeatedly. This statement will be discussed further in Chapter 7.

Figure 4-1 illustrates the step-by-step creation of the source program described above. Your entries are shaded; computer responses are not. Remarks have been added to explain what the program is doing.

Enter this program into your computer, compile it, and run it as shown. Notice that when a string is entered as input, CBASIC assigns a zero value to the real variable N.

30   IF N NE 0 THEN GOTO 10

This statement says that if the value assigned to N is not equal to 0, then go to the statement on line 10. Otherwise, continue with the next sequential statement, which is the END statement on line 40. Edit the program so that line 30 is between line 20 and line 40. When you re-compile the program with this new statement in it and run it, a zero entry will cause the program to end. Without this statement, the program would continue indefinitely.

Figure 4-2 illustrates the CP/M editor being used to load, modify, recompile, and re-execute the program.

Try experimenting with this program by altering it so you become familiar with the concepts just covered. Change the INPUT statement on line 10 so that it specifies input of two or more variables. Use real, integer and string variables; then input correct and incorrect data types for each variable to see how they are interpreted. When printing two or more data items, experiment with punctuation; use commas and semicolons to see the effect they have on display format.

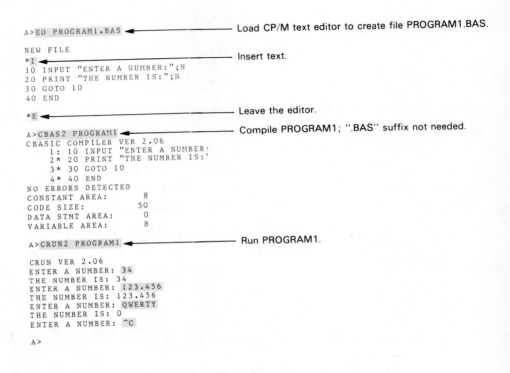

```
A>ED PROGRAM1.BAS ◄──────────── Load CP/M text editor to create file PROGRAM1.BAS.

NEW FILE
*I ◄──────────────────────── Insert text.
10 INPUT "ENTER A NUMBER:";N
20 PRINT "THE NUMBER IS:";N
30 GOTO 10
40 END

*E ◄──────────────────────── Leave the editor.

A>CBAS2 PROGRAM1 ◄─────────── Compile PROGRAM1; ".BAS" suffix not needed.
CBASIC COMPILER VER 2.06
    1: 10 INPUT "ENTER A NUMBER:
    2* 20 PRINT "THE NUMBER IS:'
    3* 30 GOTO 10
    4* 40 END
NO ERRORS DETECTED
CONSTANT AREA:       8
CODE SIZE:          50
DATA STMT AREA:      0
VARIABLE AREA:       8

A>CRUN2 PROGRAM1 ◄─────────── Run PROGRAM1.

CRUN VER 2.06
ENTER A NUMBER: 34
THE NUMBER IS: 34
ENTER A NUMBER: 123.456
THE NUMBER IS: 123.456
ENTER A NUMBER: QWERTY
THE NUMBER IS: 0
ENTER A NUMBER: ^C

A>
```

Figure 4-1. Creating, Compiling and Running
a Simple CBASIC Program

Try adding a comma or semicolon to the end of the PRINT statement, following the last data item, and prior to the carriage return. The message requesting additional data entry now appears on the same line as the previous display, since the trailing comma or semicolon suppresses the automatic carriage return.

THE DATA STATEMENT

The INPUT statement allows an operator to enter data that may vary from one execution of a program to the next. The DATA statement, in contrast, provides a program with data which is constant.

The DATA statement is identified by the key word "DATA," which is followed by a list of constants. Consider the following example:

DATA 1, 2, 3, 4, 5

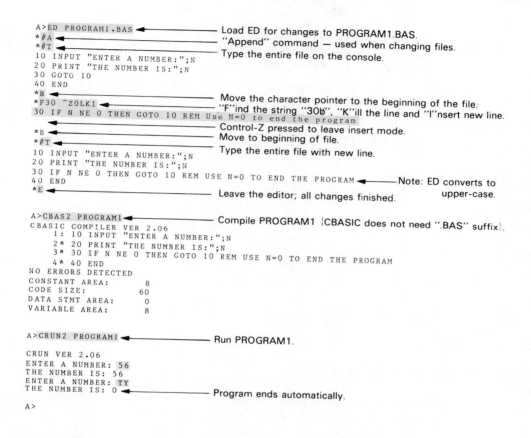

```
A>ED PROGRAM1.BAS                         Load ED for changes to PROGRAM1.BAS.
*#A                                       "Append" command — used when changing files.
*#T                                       Type the entire file on the console.
10 INPUT "ENTER A NUMBER:";N
20 PRINT "THE NUMBER IS:";N
30 GOTO 10
40 END
*B                                        Move the character pointer to the beginning of the file.
*F30 ^ZOLKI                               "F"ind the string "30b", "K"ill the line and "I"nsert new line.
30 IF N NE 0 THEN GOTO 10 REM Use N=0 to end the program
                                          Control-Z pressed to leave insert mode.
*B                                        Move to beginning of file.
*#T                                       Type the entire file with new line.
10 INPUT "ENTER A NUMBER:";N
20 PRINT "THE NUMBER IS:";N
30 IF N NE 0 THEN GOTO 10 REM USE N=0 TO END THE PROGRAM        Note: ED converts to
40 END                                                         upper-case.
*E                                        Leave the editor; all changes finished.


A>CBAS2 PROGRAM1                          Compile PROGRAM1 [CBASIC does not need ".BAS" suffix].
CBASIC COMPILER VER 2.06
    1:  10 INPUT "ENTER A NUMBER:";N
    2*  20 PRINT "THE NUMBER IS:";N
    3*  30 IF N NE 0 THEN GOTO 10 REM USE N=0 TO END THE PROGRAM
    4*  40 END
NO ERRORS DETECTED
CONSTANT AREA:        8
CODE SIZE:           60
DATA STMT AREA:       0
VARIABLE AREA:        8


A>CRUN2 PROGRAM1                          Run PROGRAM1.

CRUN VER 2.06
ENTER A NUMBER: 56
THE NUMBER IS: 56
ENTER A NUMBER: TY
THE NUMBER IS: 0                          Program ends automatically.

A>
```

Figure 4-2. Arranging a Program by Re-editing
Re-compiling and Re-running it

The DATA statement parameter list may be illustrated as follows:

Start of data list ⟶
| 1 |
| 2 |
| 3 |
| 4 |
| 5 |

Real, integer or string constants can be used in a DATA statement. A series of DATA statements can be used to create tables or lists of constant data. They can appear anywhere in a program without affecting the way the program works. All the data statements in a program are treated as one continuous list of constants even if the DATA statements are separated in the program. Here is an example of three DATA statements specifying one list of string data:

```
DATA     "EMPLOYEE NAME", "SOCIAL SECURITY NUMBER"
DATA     "GROSS PAY", "NET PAY", "FEDERAL TAX"
DATA     "STATE TAX", "OTHER DEDUCTIONS"
```

Here is the data list generated:

Start of data list ——→

EMPLOYEE NAME
SOCIAL SECURITY NUMBER
GROSS PAY
NET PAY
FEDERAL TAX
STATE TAX
OTHER DEDUCTIONS

THE READ STATEMENT

If you have a list or table created with DATA statements, the READ statement assigns data from the DATA list to variables in the program.

The READ statement is identified by the key word "READ," followed by a parameter list which contains one or more variables. Items from the DATA list are assigned sequentially to variables appearing in the READ statement parameter list. CBASIC maintains a *pointer* which keeps track of the next item in the DATA statement parameter list. Each time a READ statement executes, this pointer is set to the next item to be read.

Consider this example:

```
DATA 1, 2, 3, 4, 5
READ A%, B%, C%, D%, E%
```

The READ statement assigns each value in the DATA statement list to each variable as follows:

```
A% = 1
B% = 2
C% = 3
D% = 4
E% = 5
```

Because you can mix data types in a DATA statement, READ statement(s) must assign each constant to a variable with a matching data type. This may be illustrated as follows:

```
DATA 1, "John B. Doe", "123-45-6789", 512.67
READ N%, NAME$, SSNO$, PAY
```

N% will acquire the value 1. NAME$ will be assigned the string "John B. Doe." SSNO$ will be assigned the string 123-45-6789. PAY will acquire the real value 512.67.

If the variable types listed in the READ statement do not correspond with the data types in the DATA statement, CBASIC may assign unexpected values to the variables. A real variable will accept real or integer numeric data, but it will be assigned a zero value on attempting to READ a string data item. Integer variables will accept an integer constant; however, a real data item will be read accurately only if the value, after truncating at the decimal point, ranges between −32768 and +32767. The integer variable will acquire a value of 0 if it attempts to READ a string data item. A string variable can read any data item, because it will treat numeric data as a string with numeric characters in it.

Inaccurate variable type assignments may be illustrated as follows:

```
DATA 1, "John B. Doe", "123-45-6789", 512.67
READ N, NAME, SSNO%, PAY$
```

In this case, N acquires the value 1.0. NAME and SSNO% both acquire 0 numeric values. PAY$ acquires the string value "512.67."

There must be at least as many remaining items in the DATA statement parameter list as there are variables in a READ statement. If a READ statement contains fewer parameters than there are data items, the next READ statement will use the DATA statement pointer to continue where the previous READ statement left off. This may be illustrated as follows:

```
DATA    1, 2, 3, 4, 101, 102, 103, 267, 513, 12132, 5, 6
READ    A%, B%, C%
  .
  .
  .
(various statements follow here)
  .
  .
READ    D%, E%, F%, G%
```

After the second READ statement has been executed, data will be assigned to variables as follows:

```
A% =    1
B% =    2
C% =    3
D% =    4
E% = 101
F% = 102
G% = 103
```

THE RESTORE STATEMENT

CBASIC allows you to reset the DATA statement pointer to the beginning of the data list with the RESTORE statement. If you have a table of constants which must be read repeatedly, RESTORE will cause the next READ statement to assign constants to variables starting with the first data element. The example above, with a RESTORE statement added, would assign data to variables as follows:

```
DATA    1, 2, 3, 4, 101, 102, 103, 267, 513, 12132, 5, 6
READ    A%, B%, C%
  .
  .
  .
  .
  .

RESTORE
READ    D%, E%, F%, G%
  .
  .
  .

A% = 1
B% = 2
C% = 3
D% = 1
E% = 2
F% = 3
G% = 4
```

5
Arithmetic and Numeric Operations

CBASIC'S CALCULATION ABILITIES are the focus of this chapter. Arithmetic and numeric operations fall into three classes:

1. Arithmetic Calculations
2. Comparisons and Boolean Operations
3. Special Functions (Numeric Functions and User-Defined Functions)

ARITHMETIC CALCULATIONS

The symbols we use for addition, subtraction, multiplication, division, and exponentiation are called *arithmetic operators*. CBASIC uses symbols for arithmetic operations. The familiar + and − are addition and subtraction operators. For division, the slash (/) character replaces the ÷ symbol; multiplication uses the asterisk (∗) rather than the × symbol. In this chapter, and throughout the rest of this book, we use the term *expression* to describe any arithmetic or numeric operation or series of operations. Here are some simple arithmetic expressions:

```
A + B − 5.26
VALUE + NUMBER / 3.24
A% − B% + 7
```

A + or − sign appearing in front of a number specifies the sign of the number and is referred to as a *unary operation*. Unary operations change the sign of an integer or real variable, or they can be at the beginning of a numeric constant. These are treated as arithmetic operations:

$$TOTAL = -TOTAL$$

Arithmetic operations can be performed with constants or variables which can be integer or real numbers.

Mixed-Mode Expressions

Arithmetic calculations should *not* be in mixed mode (that is, freely combining variables and constants of different data types in one expression). An expression can mix integers and real numbers; however, CBASIC calculates it more slowly and needs more memory for the calculation. If integer and real numbers are mixed together in an expression, CBASIC converts any integer constants or variables to real numbers before it performs the arithmetic operations within the expression. Instead of using statements such as:

$$B = B + 1$$

make the numeric constant a real number as follows:

$$B = B + 1.0$$

Similarly, instead of:

$$C\% = C\% + 1.0$$

use

$$C\% = C\% + 1$$

Recall that the assignment statement assigns the value of an expression to a variable. The numeric type of the variable determines the numeric type that will be computed for the expression. If the variable is an integer, the computed expression result will be converted to an integer. If the variable is real, the computed expression result will be converted to a real number. The expression may include any combination of numeric variables and constants, with any allowed operators or functions. Consider the statement:

$$A\% = B * 2 + .03$$

CBASIC computes this expression as a real number, and then converts it to an integer, since A% is an integer variable. If A% were replaced by A, the expression result would remain a real number.

Exponentiation

Raising a number to a power is called exponentiation. CBASIC uses a caret (^) as the operator to raise a number to a power. If you do not know what exponentiation is, look at any algebra book for an explanation. If you do know, you will find this section helpful.

CBASIC uses logarithms to exponentiate real numbers, and successive multiplication is used to exponentiate integers. If a negative real number is being raised to a power, CBASIC takes the absolute value of the number, exponentiates it, and displays a calculation warning message ("WARNING NE").

Exponents may be positive or negative numbers. Since CBASIC uses successive multiplication to raise an integer to an integer power, an integer being raised to a negative exponent will generate a 0 result. If you want to raise an integer to a negative power, the calculation should be performed using equivalent real values. 0 raised to the 0 power always generates a value of 1. 0 raised to any other power always generates a value of 0.

Using BR to represent a real base, ER to represent a real exponent, BI to represent an integer base, and EI to represent an integer exponent, here is a summary of CBASIC exponentiation rules:

BR^{EI} is treated as BR^{ER}

BI^{ER} is treated as BR^{ER}

BR^{ER}, BR^{EI}, and BI^{ER} are all computed as ER log BR.

BI^{EI} is computed as:

$$\underbrace{BI*BI*\ldots\ldots*BI}_{EI\ times}$$

BI^{-EI} always generates a 0 result.

0^{0} always generates a value of 1.

0ER or 0^{EI} generates a value of 0.

Calculation Hierarchy

When CBASIC calculates an arithmetic expression, it scans operators from left to right. Certain operators have priority over others; this allows you to write a variety of expressions, but the placement of operators in an expression can alter the value which results.

Arithmetic operators have the following hierarchy:

Highest: 1. Exponentiation (^)
          2. Multiplication (*) and Division (/)
Lowest: 3. Addition (+) and Subtraction (−), unary plus and unary minus.

In an expression that includes two or more arithmetic operators, higher priority operators are evaluated before lower priority operators. Here is an example:

$$25.3 + 2.64 * 3.2 \wedge 4.1 - 1.47$$
$$= 25.3 + 2.64 * 117.79 - 1.47 \quad (Compute \wedge)$$
$$= 25.3 + 310.97 - 1.47 \qquad (Compute *)$$
$$= 334.8 \qquad\qquad\qquad (Compute + and −)$$

CBASIC calculates expressions in parentheses first. You can therefore change the evaluation sequence or the value of the arithmetic expression by enclosing parts of expressions within parentheses. The example shown above is repeated below with parentheses added to change the computation sequence and therefore the value of the expression.

It is good programming practice to insert sufficient parentheses to make the evaluation clear.

```
25.3 + 2.64*(3.2 ^ 4.1 − 1.47)
25.3 + 2.64*(117.79 − 1.47)    (Compute ^ within parentheses)
25.3 + 2.64*(116.32)           (Compute − within parentheses)
25.3 + 307.08                  (Compute *)
332.38                         (Compute +)
```

COMPARISONS AND BOOLEAN OPERATIONS

These numeric operations are uniquely suited to computers. Comparisons and logical operations operate quite differently from arithmetic operations. Chapter 8 describes how to use these operations in order to make logical decisions within a CBASIC program.

Relational comparisons are made between variables or constants of any data type. You can compare the values of a real number to a real number, an integer to a real number, an integer to an integer, or a string to a string. The idea of comparing "apples to oranges" applies here especially; CBASIC does not allow direct comparison of strings to numeric data types.

The following relational operations are allowed:

Less than, represented by $<$ or LT
Less than or equal, represented by $<=$ or LE
Greater than, represented by $>$ or GT
Greater than or equal, represented by $>=$ or GE
Equal, represented by $=$ or EQ
Not equal, represented by $<>$ or NE

The result of any comparison is "true" or "false." If you compare one value to another to see if they are equal, the relationship of equality is either "true" (they are equal) or "false" (they are unequal). CBASIC evaluates comparisons and generates only two possible results: a -1 value, representing true, or a 0 value, which means false. These are the only values which come out of a comparison; they are called *logical values*. CBASIC treats logical values as it does integers; thus, the result of a relational operation is an integer value. Here are some examples:

$$12 < 3 \qquad = \quad 0 \text{ (false)}$$
$$1 < > 1 \qquad = \quad 0 \text{ (false)}$$
$$1 = 1 \qquad = -1 \text{ (true)}$$
$$15 > = 15 \quad = -1 \text{ (true)}$$

Comparison operators all have the same priority level, immediately below addition and subtraction. You can, if you wish, include relational operators in arithmetic expressions. Here are some examples:

$$25.3 + 6.2 < > 4.73 * 1.74$$
$$= 25.3 + 6.2 < > 8.23 \qquad \text{(Compute *)}$$
$$= 31.5 < > 8.23 \qquad \text{(Compute +)}$$
$$= -1 \text{ (true)} \qquad \text{(Compute } < > \text{)}$$

$$4.67 * 2.4 + (21.3 < = 6.24)$$
$$= 4.67 * 2.4 + 0 \qquad \text{(Compute } < = \text{ within brackets)}$$
$$= 11.21 \qquad \text{(Compute *)}$$

Such expressions are allowed, but are not often clear in meaning. In Chapter 8, you will see how these logical values become more useful as the programs you write become more complex.

If you do not understand Boolean operations, skip the rest of this section for now. If you want to learn about Boolean operations, see *An Introduction to Microcomputers: Volume 0 — The Beginner's Book* by Adam Osborne (Berkeley: Osborne/McGraw-Hill, 1980) for a full discussion of the theory behind these operations.

CBASIC supports the NOT, AND, OR and XOR logical operators. They have the following execution hierarchy:

1. NOT
2. AND
3. OR and XOR

Boolean operators have the lowest priority of all arithmetic and numeric operators. All Boolean operations are performed using the 16-bit, two's-complement representation of CBASIC integer numbers. CBASIC truncates any real numbers in the expression to integers before performing Boolean operations. Here are some examples:

$$25 \text{ AND } 7$$
$$= \quad 19_{16} \text{ AND } 7$$
$$= \quad 00011001_2 \text{ AND } 0111_2$$
$$= \quad 00000001_2$$
$$= \quad 1$$

$$\text{NOT } 25 \text{ AND } 7$$
$$= \quad 11100110_2 \text{ AND } 0111_2$$
$$= \quad 00000110_2$$
$$= \quad 6$$

$$25 \text{ OR } 7 \text{ AND } 13$$
$$= 00011001_2 \text{ OR } 0111_2 \text{ AND } 1101_2$$
$$= 00011111_2 \text{ AND } 1101_2$$
$$= 00001101_2$$
$$= 13$$

Boolean operators can be included in expressions along with relational operators and/or arithmetic operators.

SUMMARY OF EXPRESSION EVALUATION HIERARCHY

Here is a summary of the order in which numeric operators are evaluated within an expression:

1. Nested parentheses ( )
2. Exponentiation (^)
3. Multiplication (∗) or division (/)
4. Addition (+), subtraction (−), unary plus, unary minus
5. Relational operators < or LT, < = or LE, > or GT, > = or GE, = or EQ, < > or NE
6. NOT
7. AND
8. OR and XOR

NUMERIC FUNCTIONS

CBASIC has a "library" of numeric functions which are built into the language itself, called *intrinsic functions.* An analogy to functions in CBASIC is a pocket calculator with special LOG, SIN, COS or other buttons which perform complicated calculations with the push of a button. Similarly, with the statement:

ANSWER = SIN(1.336)

CBASIC will calculate the answer for the value in parentheses. Table 5-1 lists intrinsic functions which you can use with numeric data. As you can see, functions require one or more values within parentheses in order to perform the function; these values are called the *argument* of the function.

Arguments may be variables, constants or expressions:

```
A% = ABS(N%)
BONUS = SQR(ANNUAL.SALARY ∗ YEARS. OF. SERVICE)
COSINE.OF.TWO = COS(2)
```

Table 5-1. A Summary of CBASIC Numeric Functions

Function	Argument Type	Operation Performed	Result Type
ABS	Real	ABS(X) computes the absolute value of X, which is X if X is positive, or −X if X is negative.	Real
ATN	Real	ATN(X) computes the arctangent of X, where X is expressed in radians.	Real
COS	Real	COS(X) computes the cosine of X, where X is radians.	Real
EXP	Real	EXP(X) computes e^x where e is the natural log base 2.7182.	Real
FLOAT	Integer	FLOAT(I%) converts I% to its real numeric equivalent. If a real argument is used, it is converted to an integer, and then reconverted to a real number.	Real
FRE	None	FRE returns the number of unused program memory bytes.	Real
INT	Real	INT(X) truncates X at the decimal point and returns a real result. If X is an integer, it is converted to a real number before truncation.	Real
INT%	Real	INT%(X) truncates X at the decimal point and returns an integer result. If X is an integer, it is converted to a real number before truncation.	Integer
LOG	Real	LOG(X) returns the natural logarithm of X.	Real
RND	None	RND generates a random number in the range 0 through 1.0. RND must be used with RANDOMIZE statement.	Real
SGN	Real	SGN(X) returns −1 if X is negative, 0 if X is 0 and +1 if X is positive.	Integer
SIN	Real	SIN(X) returns the sine of X, where X is radians.	Real
SQR	Real	SQR(X) returns the square root of X. If X is negative a warning message is displayed and the square root of the absolute value is returned.	Real
TAN	Real	TAN(X) returns the tangent of X, where X is radians.	Real

Table 5-1 shows the data type for each function's arguments; without our laboring through the mechanics of mixed-mode operations explained earlier in this chapter, you should understand that CBASIC will convert arguments to the correct data type (if possible), at the cost of lost execution speed.

Below are more examples of functions. Additional examples appear in later chapters within longer programs.

```
X = 5.23
Y = ABS (4.1 − X) REM Y is assigned the value 1.13
Z = INT (Y) REM Z is assigned the value 1.0
```

Note that in the example:

```
Z = INT (Y%)
```

Y% is converted into a real number, and then an unnecessary truncation is performed.

```
Y = FLOAT(SGN(X)) REM Y = −1.0 if X is negative
                  REM Y = 0.0 if X is 0.0
                  REM Y = 1.0 if X is positive
```

```
REM Below is a simple trigonometric function
Y = SIN(X)
```

```
REM Below is a complicated transcendental function
Y = LOG(SIN(2.0 * X) * COS (0.5 * X) − COS (2 * X))
```

```
REM Below are the roots of a quadratic equation
YP = (−B + SQR (B ^ 2.0−4.0*A*C)) / (2.0*A)
YN = (−B − SQR (B ^ 2.0−4.0*A*C)) / (2.0*A)
```

USER-DEFINED FUNCTIONS

You can define your own special functions and use them in a CBASIC program. Once you define the function, you can use it anywhere later in the program. Although user-defined functions will work with numeric or string data, the emphasis here is on numeric data.

User-defined function names must begin with the letters FN. These two letters can be followed by up to 29 additional characters; FN.ROUND.A.NUMBER or FN.LOWEST.COM.DENOM are examples of valid function names. A user function is defined using a single Define Function statement, or using a number of statements if the definition is too long to fit in a single statement.

The DEF FN (Define Function) Statement

The first step to user-defined functions is to define them with the DEF FN statement. For example, if you had to define a function which rounds real numbers to the nearest hundredth (useful in money calculations), you could define it as follows:

```
DEF FN.NEAREST.CENT(NUMBER) = INT(NUMBER*100+.5) / 100
```

FN.NEAREST.CENT is the name of the function. (NUMBER) is the argument, a real number. Anywhere in the program after the DEF FN statement, a statement such as:

MTD.PAY = MTD.PAY + FN.NEAREST.CENT(NETPAY)

would "pass" the argument — in this case, the current value of NETPAY — to the function and round the number to the nearest cent, substituting NETPAY for NUMBER. The function passes the calculated value back, assigning it to the variable TOTAL.PAY. In the DEF FN statement, the argument in parentheses is called a *dummy argument*. Constants are not allowed in the dummy argument.

Using the Function

CBASIC requires you to define a function before you use it in a program. You can use it as many times as you want, even in the same CBASIC statement:

TOTAL.PAY = FN.NEAREST.CENT(NETPAY) + FN.NEAREST.CENT(FICA) \

+ FN.NEAREST.CENT(FED.WITH)

In Chapter 8 you will see how to create and use much more powerful user-defined functions than these.

6
String Operations

ALTHOUGH STRINGS ARE NOT of any direct computational use, you will need them for more than just storing names, addresses, and other kinds of text. String operations allow you to compare and manipulate text, convert strings to numeric data or numeric data to strings, and to perform control functions. Table 6-1 summarizes all the string options available.

STRING CONCATENATION

When two strings are *concatenated,* one appends to the other; if string "B" is concatenated to string "A", the result of the operation is a new string containing "AB". CBASIC uses the plus sign (+) for string concatenation, even though concatenation and addition have nothing in common. You can concatenate multiple string constants or variables, as long as the resulting string has 255 characters or less. Here is a very simple string concatenation example:

```
NAME$ = "BILL J."+"SMITH"
```

The string "BILL J.SMITH" is now assigned to the variable NAME$. String variables can be concatenated as in the example:

```
FIRST.NAME$ = "BILL"
INITIAL$ = "J."
LAST.NAME$ = "SMITH"
NAME$ = FIRST.NAME$+INITIAL$+LAST.NAME$
```

Table 6-1. A Summary of CBASIC String Functions

Function	Operation Performed	Result Type
ASC(A$)	Return the decimal value of the ASCII code for the first character of string A$. Returns 0 for a null string.	Integer (0-255)
CHR$(I%)	Return a one character string. The character's ASCII value is given by I%.	One character string
COMMAND$	Returns the CP/M command line without the name of the CP/M program being run, or TRACE (if specified).	String, 1 to 40 characters
LEFT$(A$,I%)	Returns the leftmost I% characters of string A$. If A$ has less than I% characters, then all of A$ is returned.	String, I% characters
LEN(A$)	Return the number of characters in string A$.	Integer
MATCH(A$,B$,I%)	Look for string A$ in string B$. If present, return position in B$ of first A$ character; return 0 if not present. (See special use of # ! and ? by A$).	Integer
MID$(A$,I%,J%)	Return J% characters of string A$ beginning with the I% character. Return all characters to the right of I% character, if less than J% characters are present. Return null string if I% is beyond the end of A$.	String, J% characters
RIGHT$(A$,I%)	Return the rightmost I% characters of string A$. If A$ has less than I% characters, then all of A$ is returned.	String, I% characters
SADD(A$)	Return starting address in memory where CBASIC stores string A$. Return 0 for a null string.	Integer
STR$(X)	Return the real number X as a character string.	String
UCASE$(A$)	Translate lower-case letters to upper-case in string A$.	String
VAL(A$)	Convert the numeric character string A$ into a real number.	Real numeric

RELATIONAL OPERATORS

The CBASIC relational operators for strings are the same as those for numeric data; the principles for comparison differ. CBASIC compares strings character by character, beginning with the first character of each string. If the ASCII value of a character in the first string is not equal to its counterpart in the second string, the comparison is over; otherwise, CBASIC will continue until it reaches the last character of either or both strings:

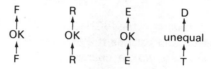

If two strings of unequal length are compared, the shorter of the two will *always* evaluate as less than the longer string. It does not matter whether the shorter string's contents have characters with higher ASCII values than those of the longer string; CBASIC's overriding rule is to evaluate longer strings as greater than shorter strings, without performing character by character comparisons. Therefore "AAAAA" is greater than "BBBB" by virtue of its length alone.

String relational expressions, like numeric relational expressions, return an integer 0 for "false" or an integer −1 for "true." Here are some examples:

"JIM" EQ "BILL" returns 0 for false.
"JIM" EQ "JIMMY" returns 0 for false.
"JIM" LT "JIMMY" returns −1 for true.
"BILL" NE "JIM" returns −1 for true.

STRING FUNCTIONS

CBASIC's built-in string functions fall into the following categories:

1. Text manipulation
2. String/numeric conversion

Text Manipulation Functions

With these string functions it is possible to find, extract, and alter entire strings or portions of them. Using the LEFT$, MID$, and RIGHT$ functions you can extract any known portion of an existing string. The LEN and MATCH functions allow you to identify and extract portions of strings when you do not know where they are.

Let us look at an example. Suppose NAME$ is assigned the string value "David J. Williams". Characters may be counted off as follows:

1	2	3	4	5	6	7	8	9	10	11	12	13	14	15	16	17
D	a	v	i	d		J			W	i	l	l	i	a	m	s

We can isolate the first name as follows:

$$A\$ = LEFT\$(NAME,5)$$

A$ now equals "David"; LEFT$ extracts the leftmost five characters of NAME$ in the above example. The last name may be extracted using the RIGHT$ function:

$$B\$ = RIGHT\$(NAME\$,8)$$

B$ equals "Williams"; the RIGHT$ function extracts the eight rightmost characters of NAME$ and assigns the result to B$. The MID$ function can extract the initial and adjacent space characters ("ƀJ.ƀ") and assign the result to C$ as follows:

$$C\$ = MID\$(NAME\$,6,4)$$

Constants, variables or expressions can be used as string function arguments. Suppose, for example, an integer array I% has the values I%(1)=5, I%(2)=8, I%(3)=6, I%(4)=4. The three assignment statements specifying A$, B$, and C$ could be rewritten as follows:

$$A\$=RIGHT\$(NAME\$, I\%(1))$$
$$B\$=RIGHT\$(NAME\$,I\$(2))$$
$$C\$=MID\$(NAME\$,I\%(3),I\%(4))$$

Even numeric or string functions themselves can be used as arguments. For example, instead of using the MID$ function to generate C$, we could substitute the following assignment statement:

$$C\$=LEFT\$(RIGHT\$(NAME\$,12),4)$$

Now the RIGHT$ function isolates the string "ƀJ.ƀWilliams", from which the LEFT$ function isolates "ƀJ.ƀ".

A demonstration program in Figure 6-1 uses assignment statements to isolate the three parts of names from strings of unknown length. The name is then reassembled and printed. The program in Figure 6-1 is listed on lines 1 through 27. Text before and after the program is standard CP/M dialogue accompanying a program being compiled and run. All operator entry is shown shaded. Note that the CBASIC diskette, together with program source and object files, is held in drive B.

Let us examine the program itself.

In order to make the program readable, a number of remark statements have been added. The first remark statement provides the file name used for the source program. Remarks are printed in upper- and lower-case characters, while statements are printed in upper-case characters only, to make the program more readable. Perhaps a better technique would be to indent remarks. For example, if

```
A>CBAS2 NAMES ◄──────────────────────── Compile the program NAMES.BAS.

CBASIC COMPILER VER 2.03

     1:       REM Program NAMES.BAS; written 4/1/81 by AO
     2:       DIM NAME$(100)
     3:       I%=0
     4:       REM Enter a name
     5: 10     INPUT "Input next name: ";NAME$(I%)
     6:       REM Find the character position for the space\
     7:          following the first name in NAME$(I%)
     8:          SP1%=MATCH(" ",NAME$(I%),1)
     9:       REM Check for a middle initial by finding\
    10:          position of the period and space following the\
    11:          middle initial; assign first name to A$.
    12:          SP2%=MATCH(". ",NAME$(I%),SP1%)
    13:          A$=LEFT$(NAME$(I%),SP1%-1)
    14:       REM Check for the presence of a middle name
    15:          IF SP2%=0 THEN GOTO 100
    16:       REM There is a middle initial. Assign last\
    17:          name to B$ and middle initial to C$.
    18:          B$=RIGHT$(NAME$(I%),LEN(NAME$(I%))-SP2%-1)
    19:          C$=MID$(NAME$(I%),SP1%,4)
    20:          GOTO 200
    21:       REM Get B$ and C$ for no middle initial
    22: 100     B$=RIGHT$(NAME$(I%),LEN(NAME$(I%))-SP1%):C$=" "
    23: 200     PRINT NAME$(I%),B$;", ";A$;C$
    24:          I%=I%+1
    25:          IF I%>100 THEN STOP
    26:          GOTO 10
    27: END
NO ERRORS DETECTED
CONSTANT AREA:      8
CODE SIZE:        233
DATA STMT AREA:     0
VARIABLE AREA:     56

A>CRUN2 NAMES ◄──────────────────────── Run NAMES.BAS.

CRUN VER 2.06
Input next name: David J. Williams
David J. Williams   Williams, David J.
Input next name: David Williams
David Williams      Williams, David
Input next name: Pilar Jackson
Pilar Jackson       Jackson, Pilar
Input next name: Raoul F. Wilkes
Raoul F. Wilkes     Wilkes, Raoul F.
Input next name:^C ◄──────────────────── Exit program by entering Control-C.
A>
```

Figure 6-1. A Demonstration of String Functions

all remarks started five character positions to the right of the first character position used for BASIC statement lines, it would be even easier to read the program.

NAME$ has been dimensioned as a one-dimensional array so that the program can demonstrate use of arrays. NAME$ does not have to be an array. Since names can vary in length, we use two integers, SP1% and SP2%, to identify the blank space following the first name, and the period following the middle initial. The MATCH statement on the eighth line of the program assigns a value to SP1% as follows.

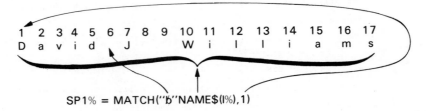

SP1% = MATCH("b"NAME$(I%),1)

SP1% is assigned the value 6 in this particular case. SP2% gets its value from the MATCH statement on line 11 as follows:

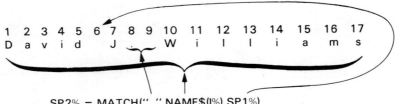

SP2% = MATCH(". ",NAME$(I%),SP1%)

SP2% is assigned a value of 8 in this particular case. If there is no middle initial, the match character string ". " will have no match and SP2% will be assigned a 0 value. In any case, we can extract the first name and assign it to A$ using the LEFT$ statement shown on line 12. The number of characters in the first name will be one less than SP1% since SP1% provides the character position of the blank space following the first name.

Strings assigned to B$ and C$ vary depending on whether there is a middle initial present. The statement:

IF SP2% = 0 THEN GOTO 100

forces the program to jump to the statement at line number 100 (on line 22) if SP2% equals 0. If SP2% is not 0, there is a middle initial in the name and program logic continues with the statement on line 18. This statement uses the LEN function to determine the total number of characters in the name. In order to extract just the last name we must subtract the character position of the blank character preceding the last name. This is one more than the character position of the period following the middle initial, which is provided by SP2%.

C$ uses the MID$ function in order to extract the four middle characters from the name. SP1% identifies the first of the four characters.

The GOTO statement on line 20 bypasses statements on line 22 which assign values to B$ and C$ for the case where there is no middle initial. These statements are shown on a single line with a lower-case c for C$ to illustrate multiple statements on a single line, and the fact that upper and lower-case characters can be used interchangeably within BASIC statements.

C$ is assigned a single blank space character.

The PRINT statement on line 23 prints the name as input, followed by the reconstructed name, which should be the same as that input first; from the display in Figure 6-1, you will see that it is. In the display, note that when more than one middle initial is added, program logic still works; however, the second printing of the name has been shifted to the right. This is caused by the comma separating NAME$(I%) from A$. This comma tabs to the next column position divisible by 20. Column 20 is to the right of the name with a single initial; therefore the comma tabs to column 20. But when more than one initial is present, the comma tabs to column 40 since the first printing of the name has gone beyond column 20.

The final three statements on lines 24, 25, and 26 increment I%, the index for NAME$(I%), and ensure that I% has not exceeded 100, the maximum dimension specified on line 2. These three statements are easy to follow but represent abominable programming, since there is no way of stopping program execution except to enter 100 names or to reset the computer. In the next chapter we will look at some additional program control statements that improve the illustrated program.

You should try variations of the illustrated program until you completely understand how the string functions work.

String/Numeric Conversion Functions

The STR$ and VAL string functions are opposite to each other; STR$ will convert numeric data to its string equivalent, while VAL converts strings to numeric data.

```
N1 = 123.45
N$ = STR$(N)          REM N$ = "b 123.45"
M$ = STR$(-N+3)       REM M$ = "-120.45"
N2 = VAL(M$)          REM N2 = -120.45
N3 = VAL(N$)+VAL(M$)  REM N3 = 3.0
```

These functions are used in applications which, for any reason, must store numeric data as text. Numbers are converted into numeric strings, which are later reconverted back into real numbers.

The ASC and CHR$ string functions convert single characters. The ASC function returns an integer with a value ranging between 0 and 255, representing the numeric value for a single character's ASCII code. Here are some examples:

```
NAME$ = "JOE"
I% = ASC (NAME$) REM I% = 74 (ASCII code for J)
J% = ASC (RIGHT$(NAME$,2)) REM J% = 79 (ASCII code for O)
```

The CHR$ function converts an ASCII code to its character equivalent. This function is frequently used in programs to identify nonprinting characters or control characters. Here are some examples.

```
REM Let ESC$ represent the Escape character
REM and CR$ represent a carriage return
ESC$ = CHR$ (27): CR$ = CHR$ (13)
```

We are going to use CHR$ function in Chapters 9 and 10, where complete input and output programming examples are given.

USER-DEFINED STRING FUNCTIONS

User-defined real and integer functions were described at the end of Chapter 5. User-defined functions can also be defined for string variables. String user functions are defined identically, using a single DEF statement, or a group of statements beginning with a DEF and ending with an FEND. A number of examples are given in Chapter 8.

7
Program Logic

STATEMENTS WITHIN A PROGRAM normally execute one after the other in sequence. After each statement completes execution, the statement which appears physically below it executes next. You can alter a program's logic by modifying the program's execution sequence. This chapter describes CBASIC statements that control the sequence in which program statements get executed, and how each statement affects the program.

THE GOTO STATEMENT

The simplest program logic statement is GOTO.

The GOTO statement is identified by the key word GOTO, or alternately as GO TO. This statement causes the program to branch unconditionally to the statement whose line number appears after the GOTO key word. GOTO can branch to any other line number in the program; remember that any valid CBASIC positive integer or real number is usable. A GOTO statement could even branch to itself:

100 GOTO 100

The statement shown above will re-execute indefinitely.

The program in Figure 7-1 illustrates a more reasonable use of the GOTO statement.

The GOTO statement on line 20 causes program logic to bypass statement 100. (Under appropriate circumstances prior program logic bypasses this GOTO

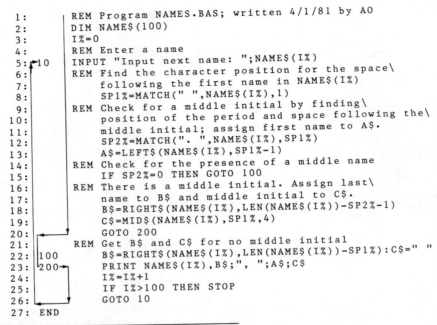

```
 1:            REM Program NAMES.BAS; written 4/1/81 by AO
 2:            DIM NAME$(100)
 3:            I%=0
 4:            REM Enter a name
 5:      10    INPUT "Input next name: ";NAME$(I%)
 6:            REM Find the character position for the space\
 7:                following the first name in NAME$(I%)
 8:            SP1%=MATCH(" ",NAME$(I%),1)
 9:            REM Check for a middle initial by finding\
10:                position of the period and space following the\
11:                middle initial; assign first name to A$.
12:            SP2%=MATCH(". ",NAME$(I%),SP1%)
13:            A$=LEFT$(NAME$(I%),SP1%-1)
14:            REM Check for the presence of a middle name
15:            IF SP2%=0 THEN GOTO 100
16:            REM There is a middle initial. Assign last\
17:                name to B$ and middle initial to C$.
18:            B$=RIGHT$(NAME$(I%),LEN(NAME$(I%))-SP2%-1)
19:            C$=MID$(NAME$(I%),SP1%,4)
20:            GOTO 200
21:            REM Get B$ and C$ for no middle initial
22: 100        B$=RIGHT$(NAME$(I%),LEN(NAME$(I%))-SP1%):C$=" "
23: 200        PRINT NAME$(I%),B$;", ";A$;C$
24:            I%=I%+1
25:            IF I%>100 THEN STOP
26:            GOTO 10
27: END
```

Figure 7-1. Logic Flow in a Program using GOTO Statements

statement, causing a branch to statement 100.) CBASIC always executes the GOTO statement on line 26. It causes the program to branch back to statement 10, which restarts the program.

THE COMPUTED GOTO STATEMENT

The computed GOTO statement is identified by the key words ON and GOTO. This statement lets program logic branch to one of two or more statements. Statement logic works as follows:

ON VALUE% GOTO 100, 50, 220, 1000

The integer variable VALUE% is called a *selector* because it selects which line number the program should branch to. If VALUE% equals 1, CBASIC branches to the first line number in the list. If VALUE% is set to 2, the second line number is branched to, and so on.

The selector can be a variable or expression which evaluates as a CBASIC

```
        REM ACCEPT AN INPUT FROM THE OPERATOR
10      INPUT "ENTER A NUMBER BETWEEN 1 AND 5: ";N%
        ON N% GOTO 100,200,300,400,500
100     PRINT "ONE":STOP REM 1 INPUT
200     PRINT "TWO":STOP REM 2 INPUT
300     PRINT "THREE":STOP REM 3 INPUT
400     PRINT "FOUR":STOP REM 4 INPUT
500     PRINT "FIVE":STOP REM 5 INPUT
```

Figure 7-2. The Computed GOTO Statement

```
        REM Accept an input from the operator
10      INPUT "Enter a number between 1 and 5: ";N%
        ON N% GOTO 100,\ Print "one"
                  200,\ Print "two"
                  300,\ Print "three"
                  400,\ Print "four"
                  500 REM Print "five"
100     PRINT "one"     :STOP    REM 1 input
200     PRINT "two"     :STOP    REM 2 input
300     PRINT "three"   :STOP    REM 3 input
400     PRINT "four"    :STOP    REM 4 input
500     PRINT "five"    :STOP    REM 5 input
        END
```

Figure 7-3. The Computed GOTO Statement in a
Readable Program

integer greater than zero; also, the selector must have a value which points to a line number in the list of line numbers following the GOTO. If the selector value is 5 and only four line numbers exist after the GOTO, an error will occur when the statement is executed.

The program in Figure 7-2 illustrates the use of the computed GOTO statement. Depending on a number input by the operator, this program displays a string describing the entered number. The program then stops execution. Although the program illustrated in Figure 7-2 is too simple to be useful, it does demonstrate a common use of the computed GOTO statement: allowing a program's execution sequence to be based on operator data entry.

The program in Figure 7-2, short as it is, is not very readable. You should give high priority to writing programs that are easy to read. Consider the program in Figure 7-3; it is much easier to follow. Figure 7-4 illustrates the same program using an expression as the selector. Variables or expressions (but not constants) are valid as selectors.

```
        REM Accept an input from the operator
        REM Print 10 minus the entered number divided by 100, as an integer
  10    INPUT "Enter a number between 1 and 5: ";N%
        ON 10-N%/100\  The index is (10-N%)/100
              GOTO 100,\ Print "one"
                   200,\ Print "two"
                   300,\ Print "three"
                   400,\ Print "four"
                   500 REM Print "five"
  100   PRINT "one"     :STOP    REM 1 input
  200   PRINT "two"     :STOP    REM 2 input
  300   PRINT "three"   :STOP    REM 3 input
  400   PRINT "four"    :STOP    REM 4 input
  500   PRINT "five"    :STOP    REM 5 input
        END
```

Figure 7-4. The Computed GOTO Statement with
an Expression for the Index

THE IF STATEMENT

In contrast to the GOTO and computed GOTO statements, the IF statement
makes comparisons and executes statements based on the outcome. Using the
key words IF and THEN, and the optional key word ELSE, this statement operates
as follows:

IF expression   THEN   statements a   ELSE   statements b

Decision	These statements	These statements
making	executed if logical	executed if logical
expression	value of expression is	value of expression is
	"true," or not 0	"false," or 0

In the Chapter 5 section on comparisons and Boolean operations, the concept
of logical values came up. The IF statement operates on logical values. If a comparison generates a true logical value, the statement or statements following
THEN will execute. If the logical value is false, and the IF statement contains
ELSE, then the statement(s) following the ELSE will execute. If ELSE was not
specified, CBASIC continues execution with the statement on the next line of the
program.

IF J%=5 THEN GOTO 200 ELSE GOTO 300

The example above tests the variable J% for equality against the constant 5. If
the they are equal, this generates a true logical value and CBASIC performs the
GOTO 200. If J% is not equal to 5, a logical false value results, and CBASIC per-

forms the GOTO 300 after ELSE. Since ELSE is optional, the IF statement could be rewritten without the ELSE as follows:

```
IF J%=5 THEN GOTO 200
GOTO 300
```

The GOTO statement which appeared after ELSE has been moved to the next line, becoming an independent statement. This does make the decision less clear; although you can still tell what the program will do if J% is set to 5, program logic "falls through" to the next statement.

Any number of statements may follow THEN and/or ELSE. Consider the following example:

```
IF J%=5 THEN K%=0:GOTO 200 ELSE K%=1:GOTO 300
```

The statement illustrated above sets integer variable K% to 0 or 1, in addition to branching as described earlier. If you look again at the program illustrated in Figure 7-1, you will see that the IF statement was used twice. On the fifteenth line the statement:

```
IF SP2%=0 THEN GOTO 100
```

causes program logic to continue with the next sequential statement if SP2% has a non-zero value. If SP2% has a zero value, statement 100 executes next. This may be illustrated as follows:

```
          A$=LEFT$(NAME$(I%),SP1%-1)
     REM  Check for the presence of a middle name
          IF SP2%=0 THEN GOTO 100
     REM  There is a middle initial. Assign last\
          name to B$ and middle initial to C$.
          B$=RIGHT$(NAME$(I%),LEN(NAME$(I%))-SP2%-1)
          C$=MID$(NAME$(I%),SP1%,4)
          GOTO 200
     REM  Get B$ and C$ for no middle initial
100       B$=RIGHT$(NAME$(I%),LEN(NAME$(I%))-SP1%):C$=" "
200       PRINT NAME$(I%),B$;", ";A$;C$
```

The second IF statement:

```
IF I%  > 100 THEN STOP
```

is used to ensure that the program ultimately will end. Since I% increments just before the IF statement, it will at some point increment to 101; this will cause the STOP statement following THEN to execute.

The IF statement is often used to test that the value of a variable is valid. Consider the program illustrated in Figure 7-1. We can use the IF statement to ensure that data input by an operator has a value that is greater than 0 and less than 6.

```
         REM Accept an input from the operator
   10    INPUT "Enter a number between 1 and 5: ";N%
         IF N%<1 THEN GOTO 10        REM check for a low invalid input
         IF N%>5 THEN GOTO 10        REM check for a high invalid input
         ON N% GOTO 100,\ Print "one"
                  200,\ Print "two"
                  300,\ Print "three"
                  400,\ Print "four"
                  500 REM Print "five"
   100   PRINT "one"    :STOP    REM 1 input
   200   PRINT "two"    :STOP    REM 2 input
   300   PRINT "three"  :STOP    REM 3 input
   400   PRINT "four"   :STOP    REM 4 input
   500   PRINT "five"   :STOP    REM 5 input
         END
```

Figure 7-5. The IF-THEN Statement

```
         REM Accept an input from the operator
   10    INPUT "Enter a number between 1 and 5: ";N%
         IF N%<1 THEN GOTO 10        REM check for a low invalid input
         IF N%>5 THEN GOTO 10\       REM check for a high invalid input
         ELSE ON N% GOTO\
                  100,\ Print "one"
                  200,\ Print "two"
                  300,\ Print "three"
                  400,\ Print "four"
                  500 REM Print "five"
   100   PRINT "one"    :STOP    REM 1 input
   200   PRINT "two"    :STOP    REM 2 input
   300   PRINT "three"  :STOP    REM 3 input
   400   PRINT "four"   :STOP    REM 4 input
   500   PRINT "five"   :STOP    REM 5 input
         END
```

Figure 7-6. The IF-THEN Statement Including a
Computed GOTO Statement

Figure 7-5 illustrates a program that uses the IF statement in its simplest form to accomplish this checking step.

We could move the computed GOTO statement right into the IF statement. This variation is illustrated in Figure 7-6.

The Compound IF Statement

More complicated decisions are possible with the IF statement by using many comparisons instead of just one. For example, to find if a date entered by an operator is valid, the series of statements makes the necessary comparisons and takes appropriate action:

```
1   INPUT "ENTER MONTH, DAY, YEAR:"; MONTH%, DAY%, YEAR%

    THIRTY.DAY.MONTH%=(MONTH%=4) OR (MONTH%=6) OR (MONTH%=9)\
            OR (MONTH%=11)
            LEAP.YEAR%=(YEAR%=YEAR%/4*4)

    IF (MONTH%>=1 AND MONTH%<=12)\
        AND\
        (YEAR%>=1900 AND YEAR%<=1999)\
        AND\
        (DAY%>=1)\
        AND\
          ((NOT THIRTY.DAY.MONTH% AND MONTH%<>2 AND DAY%<=31)\
          OR\
          (THIRTY.DAY.MONTH% AND DAY%<=30)\
          OR\
          (MONTH%=2 AND DAY%<=28)\
          OR\
          (LEAP.YEAR% AND MONTH%=2 AND DAY%<=29))\
    THEN\
        PRINT "DATE IS VALID"\
    ELSE\
        PRINT "DATE IS INVALID"

    GOTO 1
```

In CBASIC, this series of comparisons is called a *compound condition*. Actually, this series is just as understandable to CBASIC as a simple, one-condition IF statement. For you, they may take some explaining. The first portion of the program asks for input of a month, day and year. The next line:

```
    THIRTY.DAY.MONTH%=(MONTH%=4) OR (MONTH%=6) OR (MONTH%=9)\
            OR (MONTH%=11)
```

establishes a logical value based on the rule that "thirty days have September, April, June and November"; a logical *true* value exists if the month entered is equal to 4, 6, 9 or 11. The next line establishes a logical value for leap years:

```
    LEAP.YEAR%=(YEAR%=YEAR%/4*4)
```

Remember that integer variables will truncate remainders in division. Therefore, if the truncated expression of YEAR%/4 is multiplied by 4 and is equal to YEAR%, then variable LEAP.YEAR% is assigned a logical *true* value; otherwise it is set to logical *false*.

The IF statement now begins with the "outermost" tests: first, to see if the month is between 1 and 12 inclusive; second, to check the range of the year entered (1900 though 1999 inclusive), and third, to ensure that the day entered is not less than 1:

```
IF  (MONTH%>=1 AND MONTH%<=12)\
    AND\
    (YEAR%>=1900 AND YEAR%<=1999)\
    AND\
    (DAY%>=1)\
```

To make this compound condition more readable, each part of the test is within parentheses. If the month, year and day all "pass" their logical tests, the date is valid so far. The AND operators will generate a logical value of *true* (represented by −1) *if and only if:*

1. The month is between 1 and 12 inclusive
   AND
2. The year is between 1900 and 1999 inclusive
   AND
3. The day entered is greater than or equal to 1.

At this point, invalid months and years and zero or negative dates will be weeded out of the logical test. If rule 1 AND rule 2 AND rule 3 are not satisfied, then we know that the date must be invalid; in other words, the entire expression is false. The next lines of the IF statement are hard to follow without explanation; essentially, the logic is as follows:

The variable DAY% must meet *one* of the following conditions in order for it to be valid:

4. If the month entered has 31 days in it, the day entered must be no greater than 31
   OR
5. If the month is April, June, September or November, the day of the month must be less than or equal to 30
   OR
6. If the month entered is February, allow only 28 days
   OR
7. If the year is a leap year and the month is February, allow 29 days.

If the day entered passes only *one* of the tests, the day entered is valid. If the day entered fails *all* of the tests set forth in rules 4, 5, 6 and 7, it is invalid. The Boolean OR operator will generate a *false* (zero) value *if and only if ALL of the expressions are false.* Moving on to the CBASIC representation of rule 4:

```
((NOT THIRTY.DAY.MONTH% AND MONTH%<>2 AND DAY%<=31)\
```

by elimination we see that if the month is not a thirty-day month, and the month is not February, then it *must* be a thirty-one day month. In order for NOT to generate a true value, the variable THIRTY.DAY.MONTH% must have a logical false value. Performing a Boolean NOT on a false value yields a "not false" value, or a logical true. The next three conditions correspond to rules 5, 6 and 7:

```
    OR\
    (THIRTY.DAY.MONTH% AND DAY%<=30)\
    OR\
    (MONTH%=2 AND DAY%<=28)\
    OR\
    (LEAP.YEAR% AND MONTH%=2 AND DAY%<=29))\
THEN\
    PRINT "DATE IS VALID"\
ELSE\
    PRINT "DATE IS INVALID"

GOTO 1
```

Therefore, if rules 1 and 2 and 3 and (4 or 5 or 6 or 7) are satisfied, then the message "VALID DATE" prints. Notice the parentheses; they are necessary to evaluate the expression properly. Without them, the logic would read "rule 1 and rule 2 and rule 3 or rule 4 or rule 5 or rule 6 or rule 7." This is clearly not what we want; try eliminating the outer set of parentheses to see what you get.

Compound IF statements can be as complex as you desire, and CBASIC will still treat them as simple IF statements.

THE FOR AND NEXT STATEMENTS

These two statements come in pairs; they are used to repeat a set of CBASIC statements a fixed number of times. FOR/NEXT program logic may be illustrated as follows:

FOR Index = *initialvalue* TO *terminalvalue* STEP increment

> Statements between FOR and NEXT will
> repeatedly execute while Index
> has a value between *initialvalue* and
> *terminalvalue*.

NEXT

The index can be a numeric constant, expression or variable. When CBASIC executes the FOR statement, the index is assigned the value after the equal sign (*initialvalue* in the illustration above). CBASIC executes the statements between

```
        REM This program demonstrates the FOR/NEXT loop.\
            On each pass through the loop the pass number\
            and the current index value are PRINTed.

10      PASS%=0  REM Initialize the pass counter
        INPUT "Initial index value= ";START%
        INPUT "Final index value  = ";STOP%
        INPUT "For step use        : ";STEP%

        FOR INDEX%=START% TO STOP% STEP STEP%
        PASS%=PASS%+1    REM Increment the pass counter
        PRINT PASS%
        PRINT START%;STEP%;INDEX%;STOP%  REM Show INDEX% changing value
        NEXT

        GOTO 10
        END
```

Figure 7-7. The FOR/NEXT Loop

the FOR and NEXT. Once CBASIC reaches NEXT, the index value is increased by the amount following STEP (*increment* in the illustration above). If STEP is absent, the index increases by 1. If the value of the index passes the final value specified after the key word TO (*terminalvalue* in the illustration above), program execution proceeds with the statement following NEXT; otherwise program execution returns to the statement immediately after FOR.

Before executing any statements within the FOR/NEXT loop, CBASIC checks *initialvalue* against *terminalvalue.* If *initialvalue* is already past *terminalvalue,* the loop will not be entered and execution will continue with the statement following NEXT. If the value following STEP is positive, or STEP is not used, execution within the FOR/NEXT loop will end when index has a value that is greater than the expression following TO. A negative value can follow STEP, in which case loop execution will end when index acquires a value that is less than the expression following TO.

The program in Figure 7-7 illustrates a simple FOR/NEXT loop. Write and run this program, then change the values of the parameters until you completely understand how the FOR/NEXT loop works. Be sure to try positive and negative values for STEP.

Statements executed between FOR and NEXT can change the index or any of the expressions appearing in the FOR statement. To demonstrate this, insert the following statement between the FOR and NEXT statements in Figure 7-7:

INDEX% = INDEX% +2

Now arbitrarily add statements that modify INDEX%, START%, STOP% and STEP%. Write down what you think will happen with each modification, then compare it with the result.

The program illustrated in Figure 7-1 uses an IF statement on line 25 to control the number of times the program gets executed. Can you rewrite this program using FOR and NEXT statements to accomplish the same objective?

Try modifying the program further so that the operator can stop program execution by entering a number that prematurely terminates the FOR/NEXT loop. This will require adding an additional input statement that changes the value of the FOR statement index.

Nesting FOR/NEXT Loops

FOR/NEXT loops can be *nested*. That is to say, the sequence of statements appearing between a FOR and NEXT may contain another FOR and NEXT, which in turn may contain a FOR/NEXT loop, and so on. Figure 7-8 illustrates three levels of FOR/NEXT loop nesting. Rewrite the program illustrated in Figure 7-7 to include the levels of nesting shown in Figure 7-8. Your program should print FOR statement parameters within each FOR/NEXT loop.

The index variable appearing after FOR can optionally appear after the NEXT statement. This is not necessary, and is probably superfluous in simple FOR/NEXT program structures. But in nested loops it makes the program much easier to read. That is why in Figure 7-7 the indexes are shown.

Note that nested FOR/NEXT loops cannot cross each other. All of the following variations of nested loops are illegal:

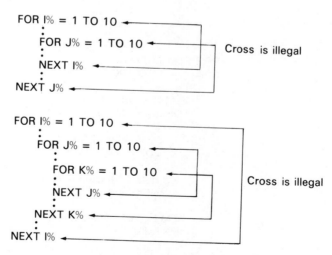

The following are legal nested loops:

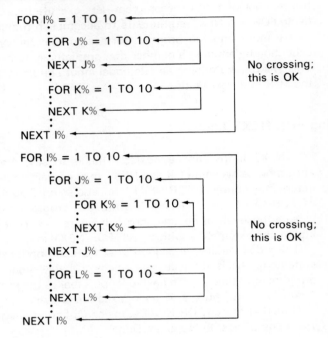

```
REM Start of first loop
FOR I% = 1 TO 100 STEP 5
    .
    .
    REM Start of second loop
    FOR J% = 10 TO −5 STEP −1
        .
        .
        REM Start of third loop
        FOR K% = 1 TO 5
            .
            .
            REM End of third loop
            NEXT K%
        .
        .
    REM End of second loop
    NEXT J%
    .
    .
REM End of first loop
NEXT I%
```

Figure 7-8. Three Levels of Nested FOR/NEXT Loops

```
      REM This program demonstrates the WHILE/WEND loop.\
          On each pass through the loop, the pass number\
          and the "index value" are PRINTed.
10    PASS%=0   REM Initialize the pass counter
      INPUT "Initial index value= ";START%
      INPUT "Final index value  = ";STOP%
      INPUT "For step use        : ";STEP%
      INDEX%=START%   REM Initialize the WHILE WEND index
         WHILE INDEX%
            PASS%=PASS%+1      REM Increment the pass counter
            PRINT PASS%
            PRINT START%;STEP%;INDEX%;STOP%   REM Show INDEX% changing value
            INDEX%=INDEX%+STEP%   REM Increment INDEX% by STEP%
            REM Test for INDEX% passing STOP%.
            REM Remember to test for positive and negative STEP%s
            IF STEP%<0 THEN GOTO 20
            IF INDEX%>=STOP% THEN INDEX%=0
            GOTO 30
20          IF INDEX%<=STOP% THEN INDEX%=0
30       WEND
      GOTO 10
      END
```

Figure 7-9. WHILE and WEND Statements

WHILE AND WEND STATEMENTS

   The WHILE and WEND statements are used together; they represent a varia-
tion of the FOR/NEXT program logic. Statements appearing between WHILE and
WEND continually re-execute until the expression appearing after key word
WHILE evaluates to a logical value of false (zero). The program in Figure 7-9 is a
WHILE/WEND variation of the FOR/NEXT program illustrated in Figure 7-8.
   Statements appearing between WHILE and WEND must modify the value of
the expression appearing after WHILE; otherwise the program loop will be
executed endlessly. This is in contrast to the FOR/NEXT statement pair which
automatically controls the repetition of statements.
   If the expression after WHILE evaluates to a logical false before entering the
WHILE/WEND loop, CBASIC will not perform the loop at all and will skip to the
statement following WEND. Compound conditions are possible with the WHILE/
WEND pair, just as they are in compound IF statements.
   Comparing the programs in Figures 7-7 and 7-9, the FOR/NEXT statement pair
appears to be much more efficient. But that reflects on the programs illustrated,
rather than the statements themselves. The WHILE/WEND statement pair has
been used inappropriately in Figure 7-9 so that you can clearly see the relationship
between these and the FOR/NEXT statements. Use WHILE/WEND when the index
variable is being modified by intermediate program logic in some unpredictable

way. To give a simple example, you would use the FOR/NEXT statement pair to do something a fixed number of times, but you would use WHILE/WEND to do it until you reach the "end," whatever that may happen to be.

Nesting WHILE and WEND Loops

Nesting logic described earlier for FOR/NEXT loops applies also to WHILE/WEND loops; however, WEND does not specify which WHILE statement it is associated with; you should make the divisions between nested loops obvious with indentation and remark (REM) statements. FOR/NEXT and WHILE/WEND loops can be nested within each other, so long as nested loops never cross.

8
Modular Programming Features

PROGRAMS SHOULD BE WELL ORGANIZED whatever language you use. It is important that you divide programs into logically self-contained modules, visualizing each as a procedure which can be removed or replaced with ease. Subroutines and functions help give programs a modular structure. Overlays let you execute programs that are too large to fit in your computer's memory. Library functions allow you to write a module once and include it in many programs.

SUBROUTINES

A subroutine is a set of CBASIC statements which a program branches to and then automatically returns from, much like a logical boomerang. If you wanted to execute the same set of statements many times from various points in a program (for instance, to print a date in the format MM/DD/YY), it would make sense to write this module only once, instead of rewriting it every time it is needed in the program. Every time you execute a subroutine, or *call* it, the subroutine will know where it was called from and return automatically. GOTO statements are useless if you have to return to varying points in a program. A GOTO statement is analogous to a rock; once thrown, it won't come back by itself.

The GOSUB and RETURN Statements

The GOSUB statement resembles a GOTO statement. To call a subroutine, the GOSUB is followed by the line number of the subroutine. This line number is the subroutine *entry point.* For example, the statement:

GOSUB 2000

executes a subroutine beginning on line 2000. When the GOSUB statement executes, two things happen: first, CBASIC stores the location of the statement *directly after* the GOSUB; second, a branch occurs to the line number mentioned in the GOSUB statement (in this case, line 2000).

The RETURN statement ends the subroutine and branches back to the statement immediately following the last GOSUB which CBASIC executed. This may be illustrated as follows:

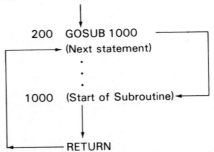

A subroutine can actually have multiple entry points as long as each entry point is marked with a line number. The entry point need not be the first statement in the subroutine. Nothing about a statement's syntax marks it as a subroutine entry point. If the GOSUB statement specifies the statement's line number, then the statement becomes a subroutine entry point. A subroutine can have one or more RETURN statements, and they may appear anywhere within the subroutine. The first RETURN statement to execute will terminate the subroutine.

Consider Figure 8-1. The shaded areas cover the line number and the RETURN statement which are necessary for any subroutine. Note that the variable DATE must have its value assigned before the subroutine is called. The following series of statements:

```
100   INPUT "ENTER CURRENT DATE:"; CURRENT.DATE
      DATE = CURRENT.DATE
      GOSUB 1000
      IF DATE = 0 THEN GOTO 100 \
      ELSE PRINT CURRENT.DATE
```

will request input of a date and call the subroutine. If the date entered was not valid, the program will branch back to the INPUT statement; otherwise, the program will print the date and the program will end.

```
1000      REM Decompose the date into three integer variables
          MONTH%=INT%(DATE.ENTERED/10000)
           DAY%=INT%(DATE.ENTERED-(MONTH*10000))/100
          YEAR%=DATE.ENTERED-(MONTH%*10000)-(DAY%*100)

      REM Set logical values for thirty-day month or leap year
      THIRTY.DAY.MONTH%=(MONTH%=4) OR (MONTH%=6) OR (MONTH%=9) OR (MONTH%=11)
           LEAP.YEAR%=(YEAR%=YEAR%/4*4)

      REM Test for legal date
      IF (MONTH%>=1 AND MONTH%<=12)\
         AND\
         (YEAR%>=0 AND YEAR%<=99)\
         AND\
         (DAY%>=1)\
         AND\
          ((NOT THIRTY.DAY.MONTH% AND MONTH%<>2 AND DAY%<=31)\
          OR\
          (THIRTY.DAY.MONTH% AND DAY%<=30)\
          OR\
          (MONTH%=2 AND DAY%<=28)\
          OR\
          (LEAP.YEAR% AND MONTH%=2 AND DAY%<=29))\
          THEN DATE%=1\
          ELSE DATE%=0

      RETURN
```

Figure 8-1. Date Validation in Subroutine Form

Nested Subroutines

GOSUB statements may appear within a subroutine, allowing subroutines to call other subroutines. CBASIC allows subroutines to be nested to a depth of 20. Nesting subroutines to a depth of 20 may at first appear absurd, but well-written programs make extensive use of subroutines, and nesting becomes commonplace. Make sure that program logic never branches from one subroutine to another using GOTO. Such practices epitomize bad programming; there is no excuse for it in CBASIC. Providing you do not branch out of a subroutine, you need never concern yourself with orderly execution flow into and out of nested subroutines.

Computed GOSUB Statement

There is also a computed GOSUB statement equivalent to the computed GOTO described in Chapter 7. The computed GOSUB statement takes the form:

ON B% GOSUB 1000, 600, 360, 2000

If the index (B%) equals 1, the subroutine at line number 1000 is called. If B% equals 2, the subroutine at line number 600 is called, and so on. In each case the RETURN statement in the called subroutine causes program execution to return to the statement which directly follows the computed GOSUB.

MULTIPLE-LINE FUNCTIONS

Although similar to subroutines, multiple-line functions have many advantages which make programs more modular. Functions allow you to send and receive data automatically. Function names can be up to 31 characters long, making a function reference easier to read than a GOSUB statement. You must place subroutines at a specific line number; you are not required to do so with functions.

However, functions have some disadvantages in comparison to subroutines. Other dialects of BASIC do not support multiple-line functions; this is a disadvantage if you plan on writing software for many forms of BASIC. There are some rules which you must obey when using multiple-line functions. GOTO statements to line numbers outside the function definition are not allowed, whereas subroutines allow GOTO statements to any line number in the program. Functions must be defined in the program before they are used; subroutines can reside anywhere in a program. Nesting of subroutines is allowed in CBASIC, but functions cannot be nested. However, a function can be called from within another function.

Are these syntax restrictions real disadvantages? You are free to write incomprehensible subroutines; functions require that you have a little style.

How Functions Work

When a CBASIC program executes a user-defined function, it "passes" data inside parentheses to the function itself. Once the function is complete, it uses the function name to pass data back to the same program statement which executed the function. Functions do not have to contain an argument. CBASIC treats functions as variables when it evaluates the syntax of a function reference.

Multiple-line functions can be of string or numeric (integer or real) type. The function name itself determines what type of data the function passes back to the main program; FN.NEW.PAGE$, for example, would be a string function, FN.PERCENT would be a real numeric function, and FN.BIT.MASK% would be an integer function. The data type of the function name does *not* limit what types of data can be inside the function argument itself. Any constants, expressions, variables or other functions can be in a function reference.

The DEF FN Statement for Multiple-Line Functions

The subroutine in Figure 8-1 can be rewritten as a function. The first step is to define it:

```
DEF FN.DATE.CHECK%(DATE.ENTERED)
```

To define a multiple-line function, use the DEF FN statement followed by the function name and the dummy argument. Remember that a single-line function, described at the end of Chapter 5, requires an equal sign followed by the function expression. The function name, FN.CHECK.DATE%, is treated as a variable which can have values assigned to it within the function itself. The dummy argument, DATE.ENTERED, is a real numeric variable used within the body of the function. By using the variables you need as the dummy arguments, you avoid having to use assignment statements to set values as you would in a subroutine call. Note that only variables can be a dummy argument. Constants or expressions have to appear within the body of the function definition.

Local and Global Variables

CBASIC treats dummy arguments as *local* to the function itself. Local variables are independent of the rest of the program; for instance, DATE.ENTERED is a local variable. If DATE.ENTERED were used in the same program outside of the function, CBASIC would treat DATE.ENTERED as two different variables: as a *global* variable, which can be changed anywhere in the program, and, within the function FN.CHECK.DATE%, as a local variable, modifiable only within the body of the function itself.

Returning the Value of a Multiple-Line Function

The following part of the function:

```
            THEN FN.DATE.CHECK%=1\
            ELSE FN.DATE.CHECK%=0

      RETURN
      FEND
```

conditionally assigns a −1 value to the function name if the date is valid; otherwise, the function name is set to zero (logical false). Multiple-line functions can contain any number of assignments to the function name. The last value assigned to the function name is the value which will be passed back to the main program.

Terminating the Function Definition

The last two statements in the function definition, RETURN and FEND, are required. RETURN can be anywhere in the function, and can be used any number of times. This statement ends the function's execution and returns to the main program with the latest value assigned to the function name.

FEND is the *function terminator.* It can only appear once, at the end of the function definition. FEND is an executable statement, but your program should never execute it. If CBASIC's run-time monitor, CRUN2, executes an FEND statement in a program, it will display an error message and abort the program. Your function must always end with a RETURN statement first.

Using the Function

The following series of statements are equivalent to a subroutine call, but fewer statements are needed:

```
100   INPUT "ENTER DATE:"; CURR.DATE
      IF FN.DATE.CHECK%(CURR. DATE)\
      THEN PRINT CURR. DATE\
      ELSE GOTO 100
```

Add this series of statements to the end of the function in Figure 8-2. Enter and compile the program, and try running it. Notice that CBASIC will *not* execute any function unless you specifically call it with a function reference. This is not possible with subroutines, which CBASIC will execute as program logic dictates. In the next chapter you will see multiple-line functions used extensively.

```
DEF FN.DATE.CHECK%(DATE.ENTERED)

REM If date entered is valid, FN.DATE.CHECK% is true;\
    Otherwise, FN.DATE.CHECK% is false (set to zero).

REM Decompose the date into three integer variables
MONTH%=INT%(DATE.ENTERED/10000)
  DAY%=INT%(DATE.ENTERED-(MONTH%*10000))/100
 YEAR%=DATE.ENTERED-(MONTH%*10000)-(DAY%*100)

REM Set logical values for thirty-day month or leap year
THIRTY.DAY.MONTH%=(MONTH%=4) OR (MONTH%=6) OR (MONTH%=9) OR (MONTH%=11)
     LEAP.YEAR%=(YEAR%=YEAR%/4*4)

REM Test for legal date
IF  (MONTH%>=1 AND MONTH%<=12)\
    AND\
    (YEAR%>=0 AND YEAR%<=99)\
    AND\
    (DAY%>=1)\
    AND\
      ((NOT THIRTY.DAY.MONTH% AND MONTH%<>2 AND DAY%<=31)\
      OR\
      (THIRTY.DAY.MONTH% AND DAY%<=30)\
      OR\
      (MONTH%=2 AND DAY%<=28)\
      OR\
      (LEAP.YEAR% AND MONTH%=2 AND DAY%<=29))\
      THEN FN.DATE.CHECK%=1\
      ELSE FN.DATE.CHECK%=0

RETURN
FEND
```

Figure 8-2. Date Validation Written as a Multiple-Line Function

PROGRAM OVERLAYS AND CHAINING

When a program becomes too large to fit in available memory you can break it up into smaller programs, called overlays. Each program overlay is stored as a separate, compiled program file. Upon completing execution, a program identifies the next overlay in the chain via its file name. This overlay is brought into memory and then executed. The new overlay can end by bringing in yet another overlay, by recalling the previous overlay, or simply by stopping program execution.

There are some restrictions placed on the way overlays utilize memory. These restrictions are a function of CBASIC memory organization as described in Chapter 12. Many of these restrictions can be overcome if you compile programs that are intended to be overlays using the %CHAIN compiler directive, as described in Chapter 16.

An overlay completely wipes out the previous program, but the previous program can pass data to the overlay. This data must be defined as "common" by the program that leaves the data in memory, as well as by the overlay that is subsequently brought in.

The CHAIN Statement

A program terminates itself and fetches an overlay by executing the CHAIN statement identified by the key word CHAIN. The overlay file is specified by its file name, which must already be compiled and have a file suffix of INT. Here are two examples:

```
REM   Exit the program; load sort/merge overlay
CHAIN   "SORTMRGE"

REM   Use a string expression here for overlay
DRIVE = "B:"
PROG.NAME$ = "MENU"
CHAIN DRIVE$ + PROG.NAME$
```

Overlays start execution beginning with the first statement in the program.

The COMMON Statement

Data passed from one overlay to another is identified with the COMMON statement, which is specified by the key word COMMON followed by a list of common variable names. COMMON statements, if present, must be the first executable statements in a program. Only REM statements may precede COMMON statements.

The program sending and the program receiving common data both use a COMMON statement to identify common data. The COMMON statement variable list identifies common data using variable names. The actual variable names used in the two COMMON statements may differ, providing they agree in sequence and type. This may be illustrated as follows:

Sending Program:
COMMON   A$, X, Y%

Receiving Program:
COMMON   M$, D, B%

The only unusual feature of the COMMON statement is that array variables are followed by one parameter which specifies the number of array subscripts. The array variables must appear in a dimension (DIM) statement. This may be illustrated as follows:

COMMON   X1, VAL, A(1), NO%, B(2), C%(3)
DIM   A(10), B$(10,20), C%(2, 5, 10)

Figure 8-3 illustrates relevant program statements that fetch an overlay, together with the overlay itself. Common data, specifications, and chaining are illustrated.

In this figure, three dimensioned variables are passed to the overlay as common data. As illustrated, these three variables have 1, 2, and 3 dimensions. Notice that the COMMON statement identifies the number of dimensions, but the actual dimension values are taken from the DIM statement. It is imperative that the DIM statement specify exactly the same dimensions in every program overlay; otherwise common data will be misassigned to variables.

```
COMMON NEWVAL, NO%, PAY(1), NAMES$(2), TABLES%(3)
DIM   PAY(20), NAMES$(2,20), TABLES%(3,5,10)
REM   Declare common data and specify a data sequence
  .
  .
REM   End program execution
REM   Fetch overlay JOBCOST.INT from drive B
CHAIN  "B:JOBCOST.INT"
END


REM   Start of overlay JOBCOST.INT
REM   First identify arrays and common data
COMMON VALUE, N%, PMNT(1), MN$(2), TBL%(3)
DIM PMNT(20), NM$(2,20), TBL%(3,5,10)
```

Figure 8-3. Passing Common Data to a Chained Overlay

In Figure 8-3 all of the variables in the DIM statement also appear in the COMMON statement. This is not necessary. Dimension statements may include variables that do not appear in the COMMON statement. It is only necessary that array variables of the same type, having the same number and magnitude of subscripts, are named in each COMMON statement. Two or more COMMON statements may appear one after the other in a program.

CBASIC LIBRARY FEATURES

Suppose you wanted to use a given program segment in other programs. You could use ED or some other text editor to "merge" the section of CBASIC source code into another program, thus saving yourself the effort involved in retyping the same portion of source code into every new program. What if this program segment has some serious bug which was duplicated in every program you merged the program segment into? The answer is to avoid this trouble altogether by using CBASIC library features.

The %INCLUDE Statement

The %INCLUDE statement is not a CBASIC key word; it is a *compiler directive*. The %INCLUDE statement causes the CBASIC compiler to include another source program in the compilation process. This feature allows you to organize a series of modules in separate program files which the compiler will piece together for you. For instance, if you had a special subroutine to perform cursor controls for a CRT display, you could write a module which performs cursor addressing and store the subroutine in a file called CRTDATA.BAS. This module can fit into another program as shown in Figure 8-4.

When the main program DATA-ENT.BAS is compiled, CBASIC will encounter the %INCLUDE statement and "park" DATA-ENT.BAS while loading in and compiling CRTDATA.BAS. Once CBASIC reaches the end of CRTDATA.BAS, it again turns to DATA-ENT.BAS and continues compiling the program. If the CBASIC compiler encounters an END statement in an included program, compilation will cease unconditionally. For this reason, don't put END statements in included programs.

The %INCLUDE directive is useful because it saves space and time. CBASIC source programs will be shorter because frequently used modules are written only once and can be duplicated in many programs. The time needed to change the same module in many programs is reduced to that needed to change only one program. By simply recompiling programs which use the changed module, you can be sure that all programs were changed properly.

```
 1: REM DATA-ENT.BAS   Data entry program; written 4/14/81 by MM
 2:
 3: %INCLUDE CRTDATA  ◄── Start compiling CRTDATA.BAS; "park" DATA-ENT.BAS
 4= REM --------------------CRTDATA.BAS-------------------------\
 5=            CRT cursor control commands for Hazeltine 1500
 6=
 7= CLEAR.SCREEN$=CHR$(126)+CHR$(28)
 8= CURSOR.HOME$=CHR$(126)+CHR$(18)
 9= CURSOR.UP$=CHR$(126)+CHR$(12)
1·0= CURSOR.DOWN$=CHR$(126)+CHR$(11)
11=
12: REM --------------End of CRTDATA.BAS--------------------------
13: ◄── Resume compiling DATA-ENT.BAS when end of CRTDATA.BAS is reached
14: REM Begin program; clear the screen
15:
16: PRINT CLEAR.SCREEN$;"DATA ENTRY PROGRAM"
    •
    •
    •
```

*Equal signs indicate included statements

Figure 8-4. Compiler Listing for DATA-ENT.BAS, With
the Included Module CRTDATA.BAS

Nesting %INCLUDE Directives

A module which CBASIC includes can include other modules; however, the compiler will only allow six levels of %INCLUDE nesting. If CBASIC has already compiled a program file which is again referenced in a nested %INCLUDE statement, a compiler error will occur.

9
Input Programming

MODULES WHICH ACCEPT data entry from an operator are frequently the most difficult to write. Because operators can enter information incorrectly, checking input for validity is a critical function of any program. Of course, once a mistake is made, it must be corrected; here is the other side of the problem. Error correction must be fast and easy if you want an operator to use the program effectively. You will minimize data entry problems if you follow these four steps:

1. Make it easy for operators to see and understand what they are being asked to enter.

2. Check entered data immediately for detectable errors. Reject invalid data with appropriate explanation. Allow the operator to reenter the rejected data.

3. Do not use entered data until appropriate personnel have been given every opportunity to check the data and correct errors. Computers cannot catch simple errors like transposed digits.

4. Keep a printed record of all entered data. This is necessary for an audit trail. Also, if your program generates improbable results, it will probably help you find the cause.

This chapter also explains advanced input procedures, which will be of use to experienced programmers.

STRUCTURING INPUT PROGRAMS

The terminal your computer uses will affect the way the input section of a program is written. For example, a video display makes a critical difference in the way data input is handled. Today the most inexpensive microcomputer systems have a video display, but video display terminals differ greatly in operation. Some allow the cursor to be positioned anywhere on the screen; others do not. Some allow a permanent display to be created, with input data inserted into the display; others do not. Some have keys that move the cursor; others do not.

You should at all costs avoid sprinkling a program with statements that depend directly on the characteristics of one terminal. Imagine combing through a program statement by statement, making a lot of changes to accommodate a new terminal. Instead, use string variables, functions, and subroutines to specify operations such as clearing the screen, moving the cursor, and so forth. Then you can accommodate a new terminal by redefining the variables, subroutines, and functions. The next section describes a program which uses a modular approach toward data input on a video display terminal.

Screen-Handling

Here are some functions which most terminals on the market will perform:

- Home the cursor
- Clear the screen and home the cursor
- Move the cursor up or down one row

Special ASCII characters controlling the cursor are often used to perform these functions. The terminal will recognize PRINT statements which contain these characters; however, each terminal manufacturer uses different characters to perform the same cursor control functions. Therefore, the following variables will contain the special characters needed to manipulate the screen display. Here are the string variable definitions:

```
REM   THE FOLLOWING CURSOR MOVEMENT STRING CHARACTERS ARE
REM   DEFINED AT THE START OF THE PROGRAM, TO BE USED BY
REM   ALL MODULES
HOME$ = CHR$(126) + CHR$(18): \MOVE CURSOR TO COLUMN 1, ROW 1
CLEAR$ = CHR$(126) + CHR$(28):\CLEAR SCREEN, HOME CURSOR
UP$ = CHR$(126) + CHR$(12):   \MOVE CURSOR UP ONE ROW
DOWN$ = CHR$(126) + CHR$(11): \MOVE CURSOR DOWN ONE ROW
CR$ = CHR$(13):               \CARRIAGE RETURN WITHOUT LINE FEED
RHT$ = CHR$(16):              \MOVE CURSOR RIGHT ONE SPACE
```

We will use the additional string variables listed below when programming the display:

BL$ is a string that is assigned a row of blank characters.

MOVR$ is a string that is assigned a row of right shift characters which pass over but do not overwrite data on the screen.

MOVL$ is a string that is assigned a row of left shift characters.

LINE%   is an integer set equal to the number of characters per line, or the screen width.

MOVU$ is a string that is assigned a series of cursor-up characters.

MOVD$ is a string that is assigned a series of cursor-down characters.

User-Defined Functions for Cursor Control

The following user-defined functions will perform the necessary tasks for manipulating data on the display screen:

FN.CLEAR.LEFT$ Clear the current line to the left of the present cursor position.

FN.CLEAR.RIGHT$ Clear the current line to the right of the cursor position.

FN.UP$(I%)   Move the cursor up I% rows.

FN.DOWN$(I%)   Move the cursor down I% rows.

FN.LINE$ Move the cursor to the I% row.

These functions are defined in one module as follows:

```
REM   FN.UP$(I%) MOVES THE CURSOR UP I% ROWS,
REM   WHILE REMAINING IN THE SAME COLUMN
DEF   FN.UP$(I%) = LEFT$(MOVU$,I% * LEN(UP$))

REM   FN.DOWN$(I%) MOVES THE CURSOR DOWN I% ROWS,
REM   WHILE REMAINING IN THE SAME COLUMN
DEF   FN.DOWN$(I%) = LEFT$(MOVD$,I% * LEN(DOWN$))

REM   FN.RIGHT$(I%) MOVES THE CURSOR RIGHT I% COLUMNS
DEF   FN.RIGHT$(I%)
      PRINT UP$
      FN.RIGHT$ = LEFT$(MOVR$,(I% - 1) * LEN(RHT$))
      RETURN
FEND

REM   FN.LINE$(I%) MOVES THE CURSOR TO THE I% ROW
REM   IN THE FIRST COLUMN
```

```
DEF   FN.LINE$(I%)
      FN.LINE$ = HOME$ + \
                 FN.DOWN$(I%- 1)
      RETURN
FEND

REM   FN.CLEAR$(FIRST%,LAST%) CLEARS THE CURRENT LINE
REM   FROM POSITION FIRST% TO POSITION LAST%
DEF   FN.CLEAR$(FIRST%,LAST%)
      FN.CLEAR$ = FN.RIGHT$(FIRST% - 1) + \
                  LEFT$(BL$,LAST% - FIRST% + 1)
      RETURN
FEND
```

A MAILING LIST DATA ENTRY PROGRAM

We are going to illustrate good data entry programming practice by writing a short program that receives names and addresses as data input. We will write this program in steps to better explain the logic of each step.

First we must decide how addresses are to be subdivided. Are the entire name and address to be treated as a single, long string variable? That is not a good idea. We may want to organize the mailing list alphabetically by individual last names. Perhaps we will need to identify names and addresses by state or range or ZIP code. Therefore we will subdivide each name and address into separate data items (or fields) as follows:

Field 1: NAME$, name

Field 2: STREET$, street address

Field 3: CITY$, city

Field 4: STATE$, state

Field 5: ZIP$, ZIP code

Fields have been identified using five strings with self-explanatory variable names.

Before we rush off and start writing programs, we must make sure that we have examined the way data is entered into each field. Names cannot be entered into the NAME$ field in just any fashion. Assuming that individual or company names might be entered, we must decide in advance how to store data in NAME$. When alphabetizing names and addresses, the simplest method is to compare NAME$ fields beginning with the first character of the field. Individual names must then be entered last name first:

JONES, ALAN P.   not   ALAN P. JONES

Make sure the program tells the operator how to enter names. Do not let the operator enter hundreds of names and addresses, only to discover that the names must be reentered last name first.

STREET$, the street address, also has an unforeseen complication. Although most addresses simply have a street name and number, many have an additional apartment or suite number. We could set aside an extra variable to accommodate apartment or suite numbers, but instead we choose to append this extra information to the street address. Again, remember to tell the operator how to enter this information.

What about ZIP$, the string variable used to store the ZIP code? In 1981 the United States Post Office caused many programming headaches by proposing an increase in the size of the ZIP code from five digits to nine digits. Most foreign countries have ZIP codes that include letters as well as digits.

How many characters will we allow each field of the name and address to have? The answer to that question depends very much on the computer you are using. Two factors are important:

1. Methods used by the microcomputer to locate name and address records on a disk or diskette.
2. The disk or diskette data storage capacity available.

Finding data records on a diskette or disk is much faster and easier if every record in a particular file has exactly the same total length. A record's address is then given by the starting address for the file, offset by the record number multiplied by the fixed record length. Therefore every name and address should have the same total number of characters. (We will return to this subject in Chapter 11.)

Think of the name and address as five variables which become five concatenated fields. A separator character marks the boundary between fields. We will set aside 128 characters per name and address.

Now consider the logic used to receive name and address data input. The clearest way of receiving this input is to display a form which identifies every item that must be entered. The cursor should flash in the space where the next input is to be received, or some equally obvious method should be used to ask the operator for the information to be entered next.

To help keep track of what is going on we will describe the program using a logic diagram, as illustrated in Figure 9-1. The "define constants" module covers the screen handling string variables described earlier. The "define functions" module covers the screen handling user functions. The "create screen display" module covers statements that create a data entry form. The remaining logic describes the way an operator is asked to enter name and address data.

First the operator enters the five name and address fields in sequence. To allow for correction of any one of the fields after it is entered, the program has a separate operation to modify entered fields individually. Therefore, statements that input data into each field are used twice: first when entering name and address, and again when making corrections. Any part of the program used twice from different parts of the program will be turned into a subroutine.

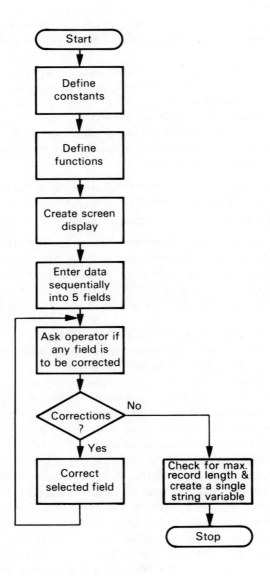

Figure 9-1. A Name and Address Program Logic Diagram

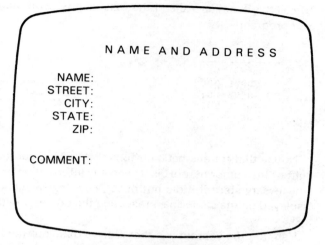

Figure 9-2. Initial Screen Display for Name and Address
Data Entry

We will use the data entry form illustrated in Figure 9-2. This form assumes a 70 column by 24 row screen. The following program sequence creates this form:

```
REM  -----------  CREATE SCREEN DISPLAY  -------------------------

      REM  NAME AND ADDRESS SCREEN DISPLAY
1000      PRINT CLEAR$; \                    CLEAR SCREEN, HOME CURSOR
               FN.DOWN$(4); \                MOVE DOWN 4 ROWS
               FN.RIGHT$(14); "NAME AND ADDRESS"
          PRINT DOWN$; FN.RIGHT$(7); "NAME:"
          PRINT FN.RIGHT$(5); "STREET:"
          PRINT FN.RIGHT$(7); "CITY:"
          PRINT FN.RIGHT$(6); "STATE:"
          PRINT FN.RIGHT$(8); "ZIP:"
          PRINT DOWN$; FN.RIGHT$(4); "COMMENT:"
```

A function subroutine that controls all data entry into the five fields may be illustrated as follows:

```
      REM  FN.ENTRY$(ROW%,COL%,PROMPT$) PRINTS PROMPT$
      REM  IN THE COMMENT SECTION OF THE DISPLAY AND
      REM  MOVES CURSOR UP ROW% ROWS AND OVER TO COLUMN COL%
      REM  TO RECEIVE INPUT
      DEF  FN.ENTRY$(ROW%,COL%,PROMPT$)
          PRINT FN.LINE$(13); FN.CLEAR$(13,LINE%); \WRITE PROMPT
               FN.RIGHT$(13); PROMPT$
          PRINT FN.UP$(ROW%);                        \POSITION CURSOR
               FN.CLEAR$(COL%,LINE%); FN.RIGHT$(COL%);
          INPUT TEMP$
          FN.ENTRY$ = TEMP$
          RETURN
      FEND
```

To call this function we add the following GOSUB statements to the screen display program:

```
REM  ------------  ENTER DATA  ---------------------------------------

        GOSUB 2000              REM  INPUT NAME$
        GOSUB 2010              REM  INPUT STREET$
        GOSUB 2020              REM  INPUT CITY$
        GOSUB 2030              REM  INPUT STATE$
        GOSUB 2040              REM  INPUT ZIP$
```

Notice that for aesthetic reasons the NAME$ subroutine clears all rows to the right of the cursor before displaying any information or receiving any input. This is a necessary step; if it did not occur, new text would overwrite anything already displayed on the same line, presenting the operator with a mixture of new and old text.

Here are the subroutines that receive data into the NAME$, STREET$, CITY$, STATE$, and ZIP$ fields:

```
        REM  SUBROUTINE TO ENTER DATA INTO NAME$
2000    NAME$ = FN.ENTRY$(7,13,\
           "ENTER INDIVIDUAL NAME (LAST NAME FIRST) OR COMPANY NAME")
        RETURN

        REM  SUBROUTINE TO ENTER DATA INTO STREET$
2010    STREET$ = FN.ENTRY$(6,13,\
           "ENTER STREET ADDRESS FOLLOWED BY SUITE OR APT. NO.,IF ANY")
        RETURN

        REM  SUBROUTINE TO ENTER DATA INTO CITY$
2020    CITY$ = FN.ENTRY$(5,13,\
           "ENTER CITY")
        RETURN

        REM  SUBROUTINE TO ENTER DATA INTO STATE$
2030    STATE$ = FN.ENTRY$(4,13,\
           "ENTER STATE AND/OR COUNTRY")
        RETURN

        REM  SUBROUTINE TO ENTER DATA INTO ZIP$
2040    ZIP$ = FN.ENTRY$(3,13,\
           "ENTER ZIP OR OTHER POSTAL CODE")
        RETURN
```

By adding the necessary GOSUB statements we create the following program to input the initial name and address record:

```
REM  ------------  CREATE SCREEN DISPLAY  -------------------------

        REM  NAME AND ADDRESS SCREEN DISPLAY
1000    PRINT CLEAR$; \                 CLEAR SCREEN, HOME CURSOR
           FN.DOWN$(4); \               MOVE DOWN 4 ROWS
           FN.RIGHT$(14); "NAME AND ADDRESS"
```

```
PRINT DOWN$; FN.RIGHT$(7); "NAME:"
PRINT FN.RIGHT$(5); "STREET:"
PRINT FN.RIGHT$(7); "CITY:"
PRINT FN.RIGHT$(6); "STATE:"
PRINT FN.RIGHT$(8); "ZIP:"
PRINT DOWN$; FN.RIGHT$(4); "COMMENT:"
```

We will use the comment area of the display in order to ask for corrections. A message is displayed telling the operator to enter a number between 0 and 5. 0 means that no more corrections are needed. 1 through 5 select fields to be corrected.

Entering 0 is an important step. If the operator enters 0 inadvertently, when additional corrections need to be made, the process of retrieving the name and address record and correcting it could be quite tedious. It is therefore common practice to add an extra step which requires the operator to type an additional entry such as Y for yes or N for no to confirm a 0 termination.

Here is the entire field correction module:

```
REM ----------- FIELD CORRECTIONS ----------------------------------

     REM --- GIVE OPERATOR CORRECTION INSTRUCTIONS ----
1010 PRINT FN.LINE$(13); FN.CLEAR$(13,LINE%); FN.RIGHT$(13); \
          "SELECT FIELD TO BE CORRECTED"
     PRINT FN.RIGHT$(13); "0 = NO CHANGES"
     PRINT FN.RIGHT$(13); "1 = NAME"
     PRINT FN.RIGHT$(13); "2 = STREET"
     PRINT FN.RIGHT$(13); "3 = CITY"
     PRINT FN.RIGHT$(13); "4 = STATE"
     PRINT FN.RIGHT$(13); "5 = ZIP"

1020 PRINT FN.RIGHT$(13);
     INPUT "WHICH FIELD DO YOU WANT TO CHANGE?"; FIELD%


     REM --- WAIT FOR VALID FIELD SELECTION ----

     WHILE (FIELD% < 0) OR (FIELD% > 5)
          PRINT UP$; FN.CLEAR$(13,LINE%); FN.RIGHT$(13);
          INPUT "ENTER A FIELD BETWEEN 0 AND 5: ";FIELD%
     WEND

     REM --- MAKE VALID CORRECTIONS ----

     IF FIELD% NE 0 THEN \
          PRINT FN.LINE$(13); :\
          FOR J% = 1 TO 8 :\
               PRINT FN.CLEAR$(13,LINE%)    : \
          NEXT J% :\
          ON FIELD% GOSUB 2000,              \RE-ENTER NAME$
                          2010,              \RE-ENTER STREET$
                          2020,              \RE-ENTER CITY$
                          2030,              \RE-ENTER STATE$
                          2040:              \RE-ENTER ZIP$
          GOTO 1010

     REM --- 0 WAS ENTERED, NO CHANGES SELECTED ----
```

```
REM   ASK FOR RE-VERIFICATION
PRINT FN.RIGHT$(13);
INPUT "ARE YOU SURE?"; Y$

REM   WAIT FOR Y OR N
WHILE (Y$ NE "Y") AND (Y$ NE "N")
      PRINT UP$; FN.CLEAR$(13,LINE%); FN.RIGHT$(13):
      INPUT "ENTER Y FOR YES OR N FOR NO"; Y$
WEND

IF Y$ = "N" THEN \
      PRINT FN.LINE$(20); \
            FN.CLEAR$(13,LINE%): \
      PRINT FN.CLEAR$(13,LINE%); UP$; :\
      GOTO 1020
```

When the operator terminates data entry for one name and address, the five fields are concatenated into a single text string whose length is checked to ensure that it is less than 128 characters. The complete program is illustrated in Figure 9-3.

If the name and address is too long, the program branches to the statement at line number 10010 in order to handle the error condition. Logic to handle all error conditions is collected in one part of the program. If the total length of the name and address string is more than 128 characters, we might print an appropriate error message before returning to the field correction portion of the program. As an exercise, add statements at the end of Figure 9-3 to handle this error condition.

MORE ADVANCED INPUT PROGRAMMING

When entering data, the INPUT statement may cause some unpleasant side effects. First, consider the string "JONES, ALAN P." Entering this string using a standard INPUT statement to accept a single variable will cause the warning message "IMPROPER INPUT — REENTER" to display. Why? CBASIC interpreted the comma after JONES as a separator between two data items when only one was called for. Obviously it is only one data item, but INPUT will not accept it as such.

To force CBASIC to accept commas and quotes, use the INPUT LINE statement. INPUT LINE is used as follows:

INPUT "ENTER ACCOUNT NUMBER:";LINE ACCT.NUM$
INPUT LINE ANY.TEXT$

All characters entered by an operator in response to the INPUT LINE statement will be interpreted as one string; therefore, INPUT LINE will not work with more than one variable at a time. INPUT LINE will not print a question mark in the absence of a prompt string, which is preferable if you use screen-oriented data entry as shown earlier in this chapter.

```
REM   ***********   DEFINE CONSTANTS   *********************************

      REM   THE FOLLOWING CURSOR MOVEMENT STRING CHARACTERS ARE
      REM   DEFINED AT THE START OF THE PROGRAM, TO BE USED BY
      REM   ALL MODULES
      HOME$ = CHR$(126) + CHR$(18): \MOVE CURSOR TO COLUMN 1, ROW 1
      CLEAR$ = CHR$(126) + CHR$(28):\CLEAR SCREEN, HOME CURSOR
      UP$ = CHR$(126) + CHR$(12):   \MOVE CURSOR UP ONE ROW
      DOWN$ = CHR$(126) + CHR$(11): \MOVE CURSOR DOWN ONE ROW
      CR$ = CHR$(13):               \CARRIAGE RETURN WITHOUT LINE FEED
      RHT$ = CHR$(16):              \MOVE CURSOR RIGHT ONE SPACE

      REM   ---   INITIALIZE STRING VARIABLES   ----

      BL$ = " "                 REM   BL$ IS A ROW OF BLANKS
      FOR J% = 1 TO 7
          BL$ = BL$ + BL$
      NEXT J%

      MOVR$ = RHT$              REM   MOVR$ IS A ROW OF RIGHT SHIFTS
      FOR J% = 1 TO 7
          MOVR$ = MOVR$ + MOVR$
      NEXT J%

      MOVU$ = UP$       REM   MOVU$ IS A COLUMN OF UP CHARACTERS
      FOR J% = 1 TO 6
          MOVU$ = MOVU$ + MOVU$
      NEXT J%

      MOVD$ = DOWN$     REM   MOVD$ IS A COLUMN OF DOWN CHARACTERS
      FOR J% = 1 TO 6
          MOVD$ = MOVD$ + MOVD$
      NEXT J%

      LINE% = 70        REM   USE 70 CHARACTER LINE FOR DISPLAY
REM   ***********   DEFINE FUNCTIONS   *********************************



      REM   FN.UP$(I%) MOVES THE CURSOR UP I% ROWS,
      REM   WHILE REMAINING IN THE SAME COLUMN
      DEF   FN.UP$(I%) = LEFT$(MOVU$,I% * LEN(UP$))

      REM   FN.DOWN$(I%) MOVES THE CURSOR DOWN I% ROWS,
      REM   WHILE REMAINING IN THE SAME COLUMN
      DEF   FN.DOWN$(I%) = LEFT$(MOVD$,I% * LEN(DOWN$))

      REM   FN.RIGHT$(I%) MOVES THE CURSOR RIGHT I% COLUMNS
      DEF   FN.RIGHT$(I%)
            PRINT UP$
            FN.RIGHT$ = LEFT$(MOVR$,(I% - 1) * LEN(RHT$))
            RETURN
      FEND

      REM   FN.LINE$(I%) MOVES THE CURSOR TO THE I% ROW
      REM   IN THE FIRST COLUMN
      DEF   FN.LINE$(I%)
            FN.LINE$ = HOME$ + \
                    FN.DOWN$(I%- 1)
            RETURN
      FEND

      REM   FN.CLEAR$(FIRST%,LAST%) CLEARS THE CURRENT LINE
```

Figure 9-3. Name and Address Program Listing

```
        REM   FROM POSITION FIRST% TO POSITION LAST%
        DEF   FN.CLEAR$(FIRST%,LAST%)
              FN.CLEAR$ = FN.RIGHT$(FIRST% - 1) + \
                          LEFT$(BL$,LAST% - FIRST% + 1)
              RETURN
        FEND

        REM   FN.ENTRY$(ROW%,COL%,PROMPT$) PRINTS PROMPT$
        REM   IN THE COMMENT SECTION OF THE DISPLAY AND
        REM   MOVES CURSOR UP ROW% ROWS AND OVER TO COLUMN COL%
        REM   TO RECEIVE INPUT
        DEF   FN.ENTRY$(ROW%,COL%,PROMPT$)
              PRINT FN.LINE$(13); FN.CLEAR$(13,LINE%); \WRITE PROMPT
                    FN.RIGHT$(13); PROMPT$
              PRINT FN.UP$(ROW%);                       \POSITION CURSOR
                    FN.CLEAR$(COL%,LINE%); FN.RIGHT$(COL%);
              INPUT TEMP$
              FN.ENTRY$ = TEMP$
              RETURN
        FEND


  REM   ********************************************************************
  REM   *                       MAINLINE PROGRAM                          *
  REM   ********************************************************************


  REM   ------------ CREATE SCREEN DISPLAY -------------------------

        REM  NAME AND ADDRESS SCREEN DISPLAY
  1000  PRINT CLEAR$; \                        CLEAR SCREEN, HOME CURSOR
              FN.DOWN$(4); \                    MOVE DOWN 4 ROWS
              FN.RIGHT$(14); "NAME AND ADDRESS"
        PRINT DOWN$; FN.RIGHT$(7); "NAME:"
        PRINT FN.RIGHT$(5); "STREET:"
        PRINT FN.RIGHT$(7); "CITY:"
        PRINT FN.RIGHT$(6); "STATE:"
        PRINT FN.RIGHT$(8); "ZIP:"
        PRINT DOWN$; FN.RIGHT$(4); "COMMENT:"

  REM   ------------ ENTER DATA ---------------------------------

        GOSUB 2000                  REM  INPUT NAME$
        GOSUB 2010                  REM  INPUT STREET$
        GOSUB 2020                  REM  INPUT CITY$
        GOSUB 2030                  REM  INPUT STATE$
        GOSUB 2040                  REM  INPUT ZIP$

  REM   ------------ FIELD CORRECTIONS ---------------------------

        REM  --- GIVE OPERATOR CORRECTION INSTRUCTIONS ----
  1010  PRINT FN.LINE$(13); FN.CLEAR$(13,LINE%); FN.RIGHT$(13); \
              "SELECT FIELD TO BE CORRECTED"
        PRINT FN.RIGHT$(13); "0 = NO CHANGES"
        PRINT FN.RIGHT$(13); "1 = NAME"
        PRINT FN.RIGHT$(13); "2 = STREET"
        PRINT FN.RIGHT$(13); "3 = CITY"
        PRINT FN.RIGHT$(13); "4 = STATE"
        PRINT FN.RIGHT$(13); "5 = ZIP"

  1020  PRINT FN.RIGHT$(13);
        INPUT "WHICH FIELD DO YOU WANT TO CHANGE?"; FIELD%


        REM  --- WAIT FOR VALID FIELD SELECTION ----
```

Figure 9-3. Name and Address Program Listing
(Continued)

```
WHILE (FIELD% < 0) OR (FIELD% > 5)
     PRINT UP$; FN.CLEAR$(13,LINE%); FN.RIGHT$(13);
     INPUT "ENTER A FIELD BETWEEN 0 AND 5: ";FIELD%
WEND

REM  ---  MAKE VALID CORRECTIONS ----

IF FIELD% NE 0 THEN \
     PRINT FN.LINE$(13); :\
     FOR J% = 1 TO 8 :\
          PRINT FN.CLEAR$(13,LINE%)    : \
     NEXT J% :\
     ON FIELD% GOSUB 2000,              \RE-ENTER NAME$
                     2010,              \RE-ENTER STREET$
                     2020,              \RE-ENTER CITY$
                     2030,              \RE-ENTER STATE$
                     2040:              \RE-ENTER ZIP$
     GOTO 1010

REM  ---  0 WAS ENTERED, NO CHANGES SELECTED ----

REM  ASK FOR RE-VERIFICATION
PRINT FN.RIGHT$(13);
INPUT "ARE YOU SURE?"; Y$

REM  WAIT FOR Y OR N
WHILE (Y$ NE "Y") AND (Y$ NE "N")
     PRINT UP$; FN.CLEAR$(13,LINE%); FN.RIGHT$(13);
     INPUT "ENTER Y FOR YES OR N FOR NO"; Y$
WEND

IF Y$ = "N" THEN \
     PRINT FN.LINE$(20); \
          FN.CLEAR$(13,LINE%): \
     PRINT FN.CLEAR$(13,LINE%); UP$; :\
     GOTO 1020




REM  ***********  ASSEMBLE THE RECORD  ****************************
     REM  VALID END OF DATA ENTRY
     REM  CREATE A SINGLE NAME AND ADDRESS STRING
1200 NAMEADDR$ = NAME$ + CR$ + STREET$ + CR$ + CITY$ + CR$\
          + STATE$ + CR$ + ZIP$
     REM  CHECK FOR NAD TOO LONG
     IF LEN(NAMEADDR$) > 128 THEN GOTO 10010
     STOP
REM  ********************************************************************
REM  *                      SUBROUTINES                                *
REM  ********************************************************************


     REM  SUBROUTINE TO ENTER DATA INTO NAME$
2000 NAME$ = FN.ENTRY$(7,13,\
       "ENTER INDIVIDUAL NAME (LAST NAME FIRST) OR COMPANY NAME")
     RETURN

     REM  SUBROUTINE TO ENTER DATA INTO STREET$
2010 STREET$ = FN.ENTRY$(6,13,\
       "ENTER STREET ADDRESS FOLLOWED BY SUITE OR APT. NO.,IF ANY")
     RETURN
```

Figure 9-3. Name and Address Program Listing
(Continued)

```
            REM  SUBROUTINE TO ENTER DATA INTO CITY$
   2020     CITY$ = FN.ENTRY$(5,13,\
               "ENTER CITY")
            RETURN

            REM  SUBROUTINE TO ENTER DATA INTO STATE$
   2030     STATE$ = FN.ENTRY$(4,13,\
               "ENTER STATE AND/OR COUNTRY")
            RETURN

            REM  SUBROUTINE TO ENTER DATA INTO ZIP$
   2040     ZIP$ = FN.ENTRY$(3,13,\
               "ENTER ZIP OR OTHER POSTAL CODE")
            RETURN

   10010    REM  ERROR CODE GOES HERE
            STOP
```

Figure 9-3. Name and Address Program Listing (Continued)

THE CONSTAT% AND CONCHAR% FUNCTIONS

The severest disadvantage of INPUT and INPUT LINE is that an operator can "crash" a program by entering Control-C or Control-Z in response to one of these statements. Try it yourself; then think about a sophisticated program and how easy it is for an operator to enter something which your program absolutely cannot control. If you write such a sophisticated program and use INPUT or INPUT LINE statements which could cancel a program at a critical point, you richly deserve the consequences. The CONSTAT% and CONCHAR% functions will eliminate this problem entirely.

CONSTAT%

This function checks the console device: if a character is ready (i.e., if a key was pressed on the keyboard), the CONSTAT% function returns a logical true (−1 integer) value. If the console device is not ready, false (0) is returned. For instance, CONSTAT% could be used at some point in a program where the operator should press any key to continue:

```
PRINT "PRESS ANY KEY TO CONTINUE"
WHILE NOT CONSTAT%
WEND
  .
  .
  .
```

Remember — CONSTAT% is used instead of INPUT here to keep the operator from crashing the program with a keyboard entry. Note how CONSTAT% is used with the WHILE and WEND statement pair to wait until the console device is ready.

CONCHAR%

This function is identified by the key word CONCHAR%. It is similar to the GET statement found in many varieties of BASIC.

CONCHAR% will wait for an entry from the console device and return an eight-bit value from the console device, which represents an ASCII character. If the operator enters a non-printing character, CBASIC will not print it. This is in contrast to the INPUT and INPUT LINE statements, which will echo nonprinting characters in a readable form (" ∧ S" if the operator pressed the Control and S keys simultaneously).

You can design a program which would accept input from the operator, character by character, using the CONCHAR% function. This is something you might do in order to detect special control characters in the middle of data entry.

Another common use of the CONCHAR% function is to detect an escape, or other special character which an operator might use to terminate operations at some peripheral device. Printer output is frequently terminated in this fashion. Here is the necessary CBASIC statement:

IF CHR$(CONCHAR%)=ESC THEN GOTO 1000

Note that every time you reference the CONCHAR% function, CBASIC will get a new character from the keyboard. If you want to test each character entered for validity (e.g., refuse alphabetic characters when a number is supposed to be entered), use CONSTAT% to test the keyboard. When CONSTAT% is true, assign CONCHAR% to an integer variable which you then test against the ASCII values allowed for that entry. You can use this integer variable for a long series of logical tests for validity; however, every time a program references the CONCHAR% function, CBASIC waits for a new character, thus invalidating any logical tests.

10
Output Programming

THE MOST IMPORTANT PART OF designing output modules is ensuring that printed forms and displays are easy to read and follow. Here are some useful tips when outputting to a printer or a display:

1. Avoid crowding too much information into too small a space.
2. Always align columns of numbers on the decimal point, or at the last digit if using integers.
3. Fill blank spaces in rows and columns with 0, ., or − characters. That makes the rows and columns easier to track.
4. Highlight information which is frequently read. If, for example, you know that a certain part of a report is always read first, make it easier for the reader by accenting that portion with asterisks or other characters.
5. Avoid cryptic headings. CUST REL B DIF may stand for Customer Relations Budget Difference, but printing the heading in full makes the program more easily understood. Redesign forms to eliminate abbreviations wherever possible.
6. When displaying text and large tables, let the display act as a window on the text or data table. For example, a screen may be large enough to show five columns and 24 rows, while a table is 50 columns wide and 75 rows deep. Your program should provide some easy method of displaying any part of this large table that an operator selects.

CBASIC's formatted printing capabilities will make advanced output programming easier. Anything which prints on the display can also print on the printer attached to your computer. CBASIC will route printed output to either device. Two statements, CONSOLE and LPRINTER, perform this routing.

THE LPRINTER STATEMENT

This statement, identified by the key word LPRINTER, directs all output from PRINT statements to the printer. You can also specify the width of the printed page using the optional WIDTH parameter. The statement:

LPRINTER WIDTH 96

will send output to the printer having a specified width of 96 characters. Initially CBASIC assumes a page width of 132 characters. If no width is present the last width assigned is used. In order to specify widths larger than 132 characters, specify a zero width:

LPRINTER WIDTH 0

This zero width will specify an infinite number of columns per printed line.

Note that LPRINTER will route PRINT output only. If your program contains INPUT statements with prompt strings, the prompt will always print on the console device.

THE CONSOLE STATEMENT

This statement, identified by the key word CONSOLE, causes PRINT statements to send data to the console device; on most computers, this will be the video display screen. CBASIC normally uses the console as the PRINT output device, so you need not use this statement unless your program contains LPRINTER statements. If a CONSOLE statement executes when the console was already selected as the output device, the statement will have no effect. Here is a typical statement that uses CONSOLE to reactivate the display when a printer operation has ended:

IF END.OF.PAGE% THEN CONSOLE

If the variable END.OF.PAGE% is assigned a non-zero value, output will be routed to the console device. CBASIC sets a console width of 80 characters; you can modify this width. See Chapter 14, under the CONSOLE statement, if you need to do this.

THE TAB FUNCTION

The TAB function, identified by the key word TAB, is used as a parameter in PRINT statements to tab the cursor in a manner analogous to typewriter tabbing. A number or numeric expression enclosed in parentheses identifies the tab column position. Here is a simple example:

PRINT TAB(15);"X"

When executed this statement will display or print an X at the 15th character position of the current line.

Notice that TAB is followed by a semicolon. If a comma followed the TAB function, then the X would be printed or displayed at the next column divisible by 20, in this case the 20th column position. Punctuation spacing occurs after tabbing has been completed. In general a programmer would not follow a tab with a comma.

THE POS FUNCTION

Your program may need to know how many characters have been printed on a line so far. The POS function, identified by the key word POS, returns the next character position to print on the current line. If no characters have been printed on the current line yet, POS will return 1. The maximum value of POS is the current line width as set by CONSOLE or LPRINTER statements. The following simple statement shows how the POS function may be used:

IF POS > =PRINTER.WIDTH% THEN PRINT

POS is useful when outputting text to a printer or video display; with this function you can determine if enough space remains on the current line to print data without having it overflow onto another line.

FORMATTED PRINTING: THE PRINT USING STATEMENT

A variant on the PRINT statement, called PRINT USING, will print data in special formats which you specify. You will often find that using commas and the TAB function to line up printed output is insufficient. For instance, PRINT USING is necessary if you want to print numbers which are lined up on the decimal point. PRINT USING requires a *format specification,* that is, a template or image of the data. This template specifies the type of data to print (string or numeric), its length in characters, and any text which would appear on the print line along with the data. The specification is a string which can be a variable or a constant. We will refer to this as the *format string* for the rest of the chapter.

Formatted printing is summarized in Table 10-1.

Printing Formatted Numeric Data

Numeric format strings use the # sign. In the simplest case, the width of a numeric field is specified by one or more # signs. Here is an example:

```
X = 123.7546
Y = -21.0
FOR$ = "######bbb#####"
PRINT USING FOR$; X,Y
```

Generates the following output:

bbb123bbbbb-21

The string variable FOR$ specifies two data items to print: a six-digit numeric field and a five-digit numeric field separated by three blanks. If the format string specifies a six-digit number and the number printed is shorter than six digits, CBASIC will "pad" the leftmost digits with blanks. Three blank spaces precede the first number 123 because X has a three-digit value, printed with a six-digit format string. Five blank spaces separate the two numeric fields; three of these are in the format string. The remaining two blanks print because the second number can be up to five digits long, while the number is only three digits long.

These numbers are now aligned on the rightmost digit, separated by three spaces. This alignment is automatic for numeric data, and it is called *right-justification*.

You can print formatted real numbers by placing the decimal point character wherever you want it to appear in the number. We could modify the illustration above to include a decimal point in each of the two fields as follows:

```
X = 123.7546
Y = -21.0
FOR$ = "####.##bbb###.#"
PRINT USING FOR$; X,Y
```

Generates the following output:

b123.75bbb-21.0

Notice that the width of the first numeric field has been increased by one by adding the decimal point to the format string. The second numeric field is still five character positions wide, but one numeric position was replaced with the decimal point; three numeric positions precede the decimal point while one follows it.

A numeric format string will automatically print a minus sign before a negative number. A numeric format six digits long will fit a five-digit negative number, because CBASIC will use the first # character of the numeric format for the minus sign if the number is negative. If you want to allow for a minus sign, you can place a dash (—) character immediately at the start or end of the numeric format string. If the number is positive, a blank will print instead of the minus sign.

For large numbers, you can specify commas separating every three numeric digits to the left of the decimal point. One or more comma characters appearing anywhere within the format string will specify this. It does not matter how many commas you include, or where they appear, but each comma counts as one position in the numeric field.

Table 10-1. String Field Specifications in PRINT USING Statements

Type	Data	Format	Example	Comment
String Fields	Numeric field with $ character	Add $$ to the front of the field specification	"$$######.##" specifies a numeric field with 6 predecimal and 2 postdecimal digits, and a $ character preceding the first non-blank digit	$ is not printed for negative numbers. $$ cannot be used with **
	Numeric field with – sign in first character position	Begin field specification with – character	"–######.##" specifies a numeric field with 6 predecimal and 2 postdecimal digits, and a – sign in the first character position for negative numbers. "######.##–" specifies a – sign in the last character position for the same field	Normally the – sign precedes the first non-blank character. The leading – cannot be used with ** or $$ options
	Numeric field – sign in last character	End field specification with – character		
	Variable length string field	A single & character	"&" prints a string field of any length	
	Fixed length string field	/ character in first and last character position	"/...../" specifies a 7-character string field	Any characters may appear between the first and last /
	Single string field character	A single ! character	"!" prints the first character of a string field	
Literal character	A single literal character	\x where x can be any character	"\#" prints # "\#\#\!" prints ##! "\\\\" prints \\	\ is generally used to print a control character as a literal
	Literal text and field separators	Any characters not part of a string or numeric field format.	"####ҌҌҌ####" Three blank spaces separate two numeric fields. "NO:###" The three characters NO: precede a numeric field	Most frequently literal blank spaces are used to separate fields
Numeric Fields	Simple integer numeric	Two or more # characters, one # character per field width	"###" specifies a 3-digit integer numeric field "######" specifies a 6-digit integer numeric field	Numbers are right shifted within the numeric field with blanks preceding the most significant digit
	Real numeric with decimal point	Place . character within # string, at desired decimal point location	"###.##" specifies a 5-digit numeric field. 3 digits precede the decimal point, 2 follow	Numbers are rounded
	Numeric with commas (,)	Place one or more , characters anywhere between the first and last # characters	"##,#####.##" specifies a number with 7 predecimal and 2 postdecimal digits. A , occurs before every third digit to the left of the decimal point	The position of , characters in the field specification is not relevant
	Numeric field with exponential notation.	Append one or more ^ characters at the end of the field definition	"#.####^" specifies printed in exponential format with one predecimal digit, and four postdecimal digits	The decimal point position affects the exponent value. Four character positions are always added for the exponent
	Numeric field with * in leading numeric character positions	Add ** to the front of the field specification	"**######.##" specifies a numeric field with 6 predecimal and 2 postdecimal digits, plus * characters in leading unused character positions	This is used in financial printouts

```
X = 123754.6
Y = 80124797631.0
FOR$ = "###,,,####.##ƀƀ###,###,###.#"
PRINT USING FOR$; X,Y
```

Generates the following output:

ƀƀƀ123,754.60ƀƀƀƀ80,124,797,631.0

Both numbers use commas to separate digits in the same way; the first format contains commas in no particular order, while the second shows commas as they should appear. Even though the number and location of commas are not important within the format string, put the commas where you would like them to appear; that makes the format easier to read.

To print numbers in exponential format (also known as scientific notation), one or two caret (^) characters should appear in the format string. Even though exponential notation normally uses one pre-decimal digit followed by the mantissa, you can specify more than one digit to appear before the decimal. The value of the exponent will be adjusted accordingly. Here is an example:

```
X = 123754.6
Y = 80124797631.0
FOR$ = "#.####^ƀƀƀƀ###.#^"
PRINT USING FOR$; X,Y
```

Generates the following output:

1.2375Eƀ05ƀƀƀƀ801.2Eƀ08

Four character positions are automatically added to account for the E, a blank (or minus sign), and a two-digit exponent. These four character positions are added regardless of the number of characters in the format string.

There are two additional numeric formats that are frequently used in accounting applications. If you write a program to print checks, you will want to fill any blank leading character positions with asterisks to prevent additional characters being added fraudulently. Also, a "floating" dollar sign can print just before the first digit of a number even if the number varies in length.

To fill leading numeric character positions with asterisks, place two * characters in the beginning of the numeric format string. Here is an example:

```
X = 123.75
Y = -21.0
FOR$ = "**#,###.##ƀƀƀ**##.##"
PRINT USING FOR$; X,Y
```

Generates the following output:

***123.75ƀƀƀ*-21.00

To print numeric data with a floating dollar sign, place two $ characters at the front of the numeric field specification. Even if the number printed is shorter than that allowed for in the format string, the dollar sign will "float" to the position just before the first digit. The $ character will not print for negative numbers. This may be illustrated as follows:

```
X = 123.75
Y = -21.0
FOR$ = "$$#,###.##bbb$$#.##"
PRINT USING FOR$; X,Y
```

Generates the following output:

bbb$123.75bbbb-21.00

A single numeric format string cannot have preceding asterisks and a $ sign at the same time. To get around this, use a statement such as this:

```
X = 123.75
Y = -21.0
FOR$ = "$**,###.##bbb$**#.##"
PRINT USING FOR$; X,Y
```

Generates the following output:

$**123.75bbb$*-21.00

By using the single dollar sign as text which would appear alongside the numeric data, you will achieve the same effect.

The following general rules apply to all formatted numeric data:

1. When post-decimal digits will not fit into a numeric field, the number is rounded off to fit the format.
2. Leading zeros are replaced by blank characters.
3. Minus signs will print before negative numbers unless otherwise specified in the format string.
4. For numbers that are less than 1 a single 0 is printed to the left of a decimal point.
5. The width of a numeric field as specified by the number of # characters includes spaces for signs, commas, decimal points, and digits. The only exception is exponential format, where four character positions are always added to accommodate the exponent printout.
6. When a number is too large to fit into a numeric field and leading digits need to be truncated, a % sign is output followed by the number in its full form. This will cause subsequent formatting to be distorted, since the oversize number occupies more character positions than were set aside for it.

Printing Formatted Strings

Three formats are available for printing strings: fixed-length, variable-length and the first character only.

A single ampersand character denotes the format for a variable-length string. This may be illustrated as follows:

```
A$ = MARY
B$ = BROWN
FOR$ = ''&.ƅ&''
PRINT USING FOR$; A$,B$
```

Generates the following output:

MARY.ƅBROWN

Fixed-length string formats are specified by slash characters (/) appearing in the first and last character position. If the format is more than two character positions wide, any other characters may appear between the two / characters. This may be illustrated as follows:

```
A$ = MARY
B$ = BROWN
FOR$ = ''/FFFF/.ƅ/LLLLLL/''
PRINT USING FOR$; A$,B$
```

Generates the following output:

MARYƅƅ.ƅBROWN

In the illustration above, two fixed-length strings have been specified; the first has six character positions, the second has eight character positions. The F and L fill characters could be replaced by any other characters. Strings are always *left-justified;* that is, if the format string is longer than the data printed, blanks will fill the unused space to the right. If the string is too long to fit within the specified field, excess rightmost characters are truncated.

You can specify a format string which will only print the first character of a string data item, using the exclamation point (!) character. This may be illustrated as follows:

```
A$ = MARY
B$ = JANE
C$ = BROWN
FOR$ = ''&ƅ!.ƅ&''
PRINT USING FOR$; A$,B$,C$
```

Generates the following output:

MARYƅJ.ƅBROWN

Note that the ! prints the first character of string variable B$.

Placing Text in Format Strings

PRINT USING allows constant text data (called *literal text*) within the format string. Because the #, &, $, *, and ! characters have special meaning as format string characters, CBASIC will still allow these characters within the format string to appear as literals.

The # sign is frequently used to specify an item number. Using the \ character you can generate a # sign directly preceding a number as follows:

```
X = 31
FOR$ = "ITEM\###"
PRINT USING FOR$; X
```

Generates the following output:

```
ITEM #31
```

A backslash character (\) causes CBASIC to ignore the meaning of the following character as part of a format string, and print it as any literal text. Although the # character normally specifies a numeric format, the preceding backslash will print the # character instead. Similarly, the combination \\ will cause a \ character to be printed literally.

CONSOLE OUTPUT PROGRAMMING

Consider the mailing list data entry program in Chapter 9. It is possible to add an output module which would display names and addresses entered by the input program. For the moment we will ignore program steps needed to store these names and addresses on a diskette and to retrieve them from the diskette. The following few statements will display a single name and address, and then ask the operator to type Y to continue:

```
        REM DISPLAY A NAME AND ADDRESS
        PRINT CLEAR$;             \     CLEAR THE SCREEN AND
            FN.DOWN$(3)           REM   POSITION TO START THE DISPLAY
        PRINT "  NAME: ";NAME$
        PRINT "STREET: ";STREET$
        PRINT "  CITY: ";CITY$
        PRINT " STATE: ";STATE$;\
            TAB(20); "ZIP: ";ZIP$
200.1   INPUT "TYPE Y TO CONTINUE: ";Y$
        IF Y$ NE "Y" THEN         \     ONLY ACCEPT A Y
            PRINT CR$; UP$:       \     CHARACTER INPUT
            GOTO 200.1
```

This illustration uses the screen-handling characters and functions that were defined in Chapter 9.

If a character other than Y is entered, program logic branches to statement 200.1. What happens when the operator types Y to continue? Here are some possibilities:

1. Display the next sequential name and address.

2. Display the previous name and address.
3. Have the operator enter one or more fields of a name and address; display the next name and address with fields that match the operator entry.
4. Display a block of names and addresses within given boundaries. For example, the operator might specify all addresses be displayed with ZIP codes in the range 94000 through 94999.
5. Fill the screen with names and addresses, instead of displaying them one at a time.
6. Display only the name and address fields which the operator specifies.

A well-written display program will provide an operator with such options. After you have learned how to store names and addresses on a diskette and then to retrieve them, return to this chapter, and as an exercise write programs that provide the operator with the continuation options listed above.

Consider next a slightly more complex display; employee payroll records are to be displayed as a 40-column screen as illustrated in Figure 10-1. The employee name, pay type, gross and net pay are displayed. For the moment, assume that this limit on screen width is real and cannot be modified.

Rightmost characters of the employee name will be truncated if the name is more than 13 characters wide. The pay type includes a single letter and a two-digit number. The letter portion of the pay code could be E for exempt, or N for nonexempt. The two-digit number will probably represent the way (or ways) in which the employee gets paid (e.g., salary, hourly, piece rate, commission earning, etc.).

The following program assumes a 24-row display, therefore 21 employee records are displayed to fill a screen:

```
      REM   ABBREVIATED EMPLOYEE RECORDS DISPLAY
      REM   DD%, MM%, AND YY% ARE THE DAY, MONTH AND
      REM   YEAR FOR THE DATE
      REM   NAME$ IS THE EMPLOYEE NAME
      REM   TYPE$ IS THE EMPLOYEE TYPE LETTER
      REM   TYPE% IS THE EMPLOYEE TYPE NUMBER
      REM   GROSS IS THE EMPLOYEE GROSS PAY
      REM   NET   IS THE EMPLOYEE NET PAY
      REM   FIRST CLEAR THE SCREEN AND DISPLAY THE HEADER
5000  PRINT CLEAR$;
      PRINT USING "DATE: ##/##/##"; MM%,DD%,YY%;
      PRINT TAB(39)
      PRINT TAB(13); "PAYROLL RECORDS"
      PRINT "EMPLOYEE NAME TYPE   GROSS    NET      "
      FOR I% = 1 TO 21                    REM  DISPLAY 21 RECORDS
      GOSUB 2000                          REM  FETCH NEXT EMPLOYEE RECORD
      PRINT USING\
            "/EMPLOYEE NM/ !\-## ####.## ####.##";\
            NAME$,TYPE$,TYPE%,GROSS,NET
      NEXT I%
```

Employee records are fetched by calling a subroutine beginning at statement

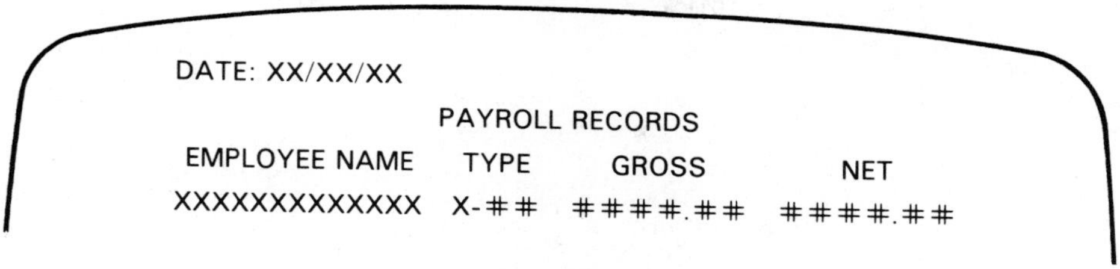

```
DATE: XX/XX/XX

              PAYROLL RECORDS
EMPLOYEE NAME   TYPE     GROSS        NET
XXXXXXXXXXXXX  X-##   ####.##     ####.##
```

X represents displayed characters
represents displayed numbers

Figure 10-1. A Simple Payroll Display

2000. This subroutine will probably read records from a diskette using programming techniques described in Chapter 11. For now, we can write a correct console display module. Since the file-handling would take place in another module, it isn't presumptuous to write one module without knowing how to write another.

Carefully examine the PRINT USING statement that displays employee records. Make sure that you understand the way record formats have been specified.

What happens when more than 21 records need to be displayed? The best solution is to scroll vertically, holding onto the top three display lines. The rest of the screen could scroll vertically, with the top record disappearing, a new record appearing at the bottom of the screen, and all intermediate records moving up one row. But make sure the operator has time to read new records as they appear at the bottom of the screen. Also, the operator should be allowed to stop scrolling by pressing an appropriate key.

Many display terminals automatically scroll vertically when the cursor reaches the last row of the display. We will assume that our display acts in this fashion. Therefore each time a new employee record is fetched after the screen has been filled, we do not have to write a program to cause vertical scrolling, but we must redisplay the top three lines. The following statements, modified from the previous example, will do the job:

```
      REM   ABBREVIATED EMPLOYEE RECORDS DISPLAY
      REM   DD%, MM%, AND YY% ARE THE DAY, MONTH AND
      REM   YEAR FOR THE DATE
      REM   NAME$ IS THE EMPLOYEE NAME
      REM   TYPE$ IS THE EMPLOYEE TYPE LETTER
      REM   TYPE% IS THE EMPLOYEE TYPE NUMBER
      REM   GROSS IS THE EMPLOYEE GROSS PAY
      REM   NET   IS THE EMPLOYEE NET PAY
      REM   FIRST CLEAR THE SCREEN AND DISPLAY THE HEADER
5000  PRINT HOME$;
      PRINT USING "DATE: ##/##/##"; MM%,DD%,YY%;
      PRINT TAB (39)
      PRINT TAB(13); "PAYROLL RECORDS";TAB(39)
      PRINT "EMPLOYEE NAME TYPE   GROSS     NET       "
      RETURN
```

```
5010      GOSUB 5000                              REM DISPLAY THE HEADINGS
          FOR I% = 1 TO 21                        REM  DISPLAY 21 RECORDS
          GOSUB 2000                              REM  FETCH NEXT EMPLOYEE RECORD
          GOSUB 6000                              REM  DISPLAY NEXT RECORD
          NEXT I%
          REM  WAIT BEFORE READING NEXT RECORD
          FOR I%=1 TO 100:NEXT I%                 REM DELAY SHORTLY AFTER DISPLAY
5020      GOSUB 2000                              REM  FETCH NEXT EMPLOYEE RECORD
          GOSUB 6000                              REM  DISPLAY THE NEXT RECORD
          GOSUB 5000                              REM  RE-CREATE THE HEADER
          PRINT FN.DOWN$(20)
          GOTO 5020
          REM  SUBROUTINE TO DISPLAY A SINGLE RECORD
6000      PRINT USING\
                  "/EMPLOYEE NM/ !\-## ####.## ####.##";\
                  NAME$,TYPE$,TYPE%,GROSS,NET
          RETURN
```

The module illustrated above begins at line 5010. We have converted the statements that display the top three lines of the screen into a subroutine, leaving them at the beginning of the program. We have also made a subroutine out of the PRINT USING statement that displays each employee record. This is a long statement requiring a lot of memory space. We do not want it to appear twice within our short program.

The method we have used to scroll vertically is dependent on the characteristics of the display. Many displays do not automatically scroll vertically. What if the display continues to output records on the bottom row? Or worse, what if it wraps around, moving from the bottom row to the top row? In each case your program will have to handle the entire scrolling operation. That may or may not be a simple task, depending on the terminal you are working with.

PRINTER OUTPUT PROGRAMMING

Programming printer output is relatively simple. Every printer, even the most primitive teletype, will accept certain control characters. Some printers will skip to the top of a new page; others have an option to print expanded or compressed characters. Many printers will accept varied paper sizes if they have a forms tractor. You should look over the technical or operations manual for the printer on your computer and find out what options you have to make printed output easier to read. There are, however, two points to bear in mind:

1. Any printer output program section must begin with an LPRINTER statement; it must end with a CONSOLE statement.

2. Depending on the printer you are actually using, such things as form feed control, lines per page, and characters per line may have to be specified within your program, or they may be specified by

appropriate switches at the printer. If the program makes these specifications, then you must read the printer manual in order to determine the characters which the printer needs and how they should be output. If printer switches are used, you should make sure that the operator is given suitable instructions to prepare the printer for the output as generated by the program.

11
File Handling

THE RECORDING SURFACE of a diskette is divided into a number of concentric tracks. Each track is further divided into sectors. The number of sectors on a diskette surface varies from one microcomputer to the next, but typically there will be two thousand or more sectors per diskette.

Information is stored on the diskette surface in sector increments. One sector is the smallest unit of information that can be written or read in a single diskette access. However, for the benefit of the programmer, information is organized as "files" on the diskette surface. A short file may occupy only one sector. A long file may require many sectors. In either case, a "file directory" is maintained on the diskette surface. The file directory lists file names, together with the location of each sector assigned to the file.

CBASIC FILE ORGANIZATION

CBASIC and the CP/M operating system look at diskette data files differently. CP/M is responsible for maintaining the entire physical surface of the disk, organizing data files in a directory, and allocating space to the data files which need it. CP/M's role is rather janitorial; the operating system takes on the drudgery and cleanup jobs assigned to it by languages like CBASIC.

CBASIC organizes diskette data files into *records*. Each record contains one or more data items. Each data item within a record is called a *field*. Figure 11-1 illustrates the way a mailing list data file could be divided into records and fields.

$$
\text{Record } N-1 \begin{cases} \text{Field 1: Name} \\ \text{Field 2: Street} \\ \text{Field 3: City} \\ \text{Field 4: State} \\ \text{Field 5: ZIP} \end{cases}
$$

$$
\text{Record } N \begin{cases} \text{Field 1: Name} \\ \text{Field 2: Street} \\ \text{Field 3: City} \\ \text{Field 4: State} \\ \text{Field 5: ZIP} \end{cases}
$$

$$
\text{Record } N+1 \begin{cases} \text{Field 1: Name} \\ \text{Field 2: Street} \\ \text{Field 3: City} \\ \text{Field 4: State} \\ \text{Field 5: ZIP} \end{cases}
$$

etc

FIGURE 11-1. Fields and Records in a Data File

With CP/M handling all of the maintenance tasks, you can forget about the physical organization of each sector on the disk; concern yourself instead with the concepts of records and fields.

Sequential and Relative Data Files

Two types of CBASIC data files exist: sequential data files and relative data files. Variable amounts of diskette space are assigned to each record of a sequential file. Each record is assigned as much diskette space as it needs. No blank space separates one record from the next. Relative data files assign a fixed space to each record of a file. Figure 11-2 illustrates records stored in relative and sequential files. Let us examine how these two file structures utilize disk space differently for the four records illustrated.

The record lengths shown for the sequential file are variable, and equal to the sum of the lengths of each field within the data record. For example, record $m-1$ occupies 70 bytes. Record m is 80 bytes long, record $m+1$ occupies 50 bytes, and so on. The same data stored in a relative file would allow 90 bytes of diskette surface for each and every record in the file. Therefore, 20 bytes of record $m-1$ would be left unused; 10 bytes of record m, and 40 bytes of record $m+1$ would be vacant. However, record $m+2$ would use almost all of the allocated space.

a. Relative file

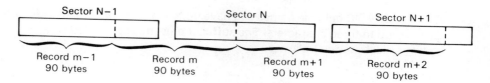

b. Sequential file

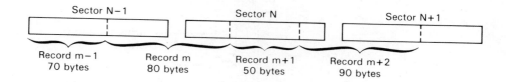

Arbitrary record lengths have been selected for this illustration.

FIGURE 11-2. CBASIC Records and CP/M Sectors
for Relative and Sequential Files

The critical difference between relative and sequential files is that it is possible to directly access any record of a relative file no matter where it exists in the data file. This is not possible for a sequential file, since sequential files will not always have the same record length. Records of a sequential file must be accessed sequentially, beginning with the first record of the file, hence the name "sequential file." To reach the fifth record of a sequential file, for example, CBASIC must first read records 1 through 4; there is no other way of determining where record 5 begins. In contrast, CBASIC can calculate the exact location for any record in a relative file, jumping straight to the the 25th record of the file, for example.

Relative files have a further advantage: you can read a record from a relative file, change it, and write it back. You cannot read, modify, or write back a record from a sequential file, since any change in record length would cause problems for the rest of the file.

But sequential files use less diskette space. A relative file assigns every record the diskette space required by the longest record; all shorter records waste diskette space. No diskette space is wasted by a sequential file, since each record is allocated the exact amount of diskette space that the record requires.

FILE NAMES

CBASIC data file names can have up to eight characters, with an optional suffix of up to three characters. The suffix, if present, is preceded by a period. This may be illustrated as follows:

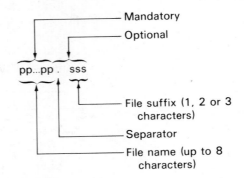

None of the following characters can be used anywhere in the file name or file suffix:

> < .<, ; : = ? * ( )

The file name suffix should be used as follows when programming in CBASIC:

.BAS	a CBASIC source program file
.BAK	a backup copy of the source program file
.INT	a compiled CBASIC program file
.$$$	a temporary file

The suffixes .BAS and .INT are required for CBASIC program files. The other suffixes are recommended, but not required. Here are some examples of valid file names:

```
A
A.$$$
A.BAS
A.BAK
FILENAME
PAYROLL.NEW
PAYROLL.OLD
PAYROLL.$$$
FILE.1
FILE.A
FILE.3$
```

Other types of file names may be used. We will explain their uses later in this chapter.

Diskette Drive Designation

When two or more diskette drives are connected to your microcomputer system, you specify the drive on which the file is located using the letters A, B, C, or D, followed by a colon. The drive specification precedes the file name. Thus a file on drive B might be specified as B:MAIL.BAS, while the same file name would be specified as A:MAIL.BAS if it were on drive A.

Usually you do not have to specify drive A since CP/M normally assumes that a file is on drive A if no drive was specified. Some microcomputer systems let you change this assumed drive specification. To avoid unnecessary trouble, specify which diskette drive the file will reside on.

USING FILES IN A CBASIC PROGRAM

A program cannot simply name a file and then start reading its contents or writing to it. First the file must be opened. When CBASIC opens a file, it uses CP/M to read the disk, retrieving information about the file from the directory. Once this information is received from the operating system, CBASIC prepares memory buffers which will pass data to and from the disk in later read or write operations.

When a CBASIC program reads data from an open file, CP/M passes one sector of data to the memory buffer which CBASIC has set aside for the open file. The CBASIC program then reads this data out of the memory buffer, as it would read and use any other data in memory. When a CBASIC program writes to an open file, the data gets written to the file's memory buffer. No data is written to the diskette until the memory buffer is full; then the data is written to the diskette sector by sector. When data is written to an open file, CP/M provides additional file space when needed.

An open file should be closed after all file accesses have been completed. This is absolutely necessary if data was written to the file. Two things happen when a CBASIC data file closes: first, any remaining data in the file's memory buffer is written to the diskette, even if the buffer is not full; next, CP/M takes over and updates its directory information for the file on the diskette. If you do not close a file after writing data to it, then data partially filling the buffer will never reach the diskette, and directory information for the file, as stored on the diskette, will be incorrect.

CBASIC Statements for Opening Data Files

Files can be opened using the OPEN, CREATE, and FILE statements.

The OPEN statement opens a file which is already in the diskette directory. The CREATE statement deletes any file with the same name, creates a new file on the directory, and then opens it. The FILE statement opens a file if it already exists, but creates the file and then opens it if it does not currently exist.

OPEN and CREATE Statements

The OPEN and CREATE statements have identical syntax, therefore we will describe them together.

To open a sequential file, two parameters are required: the name of the file being opened (or created) and a number between 1 and 20. This number is the *file number,* used later to identify the file being accessed. The following statement opens a sequential file named PAYROLL.NEW on drive B and assigns it file number 3:

```
OPEN "B:PAYROLL.NEW"   AS 3
```

The number 3, not the name PAYROLL.NEW, is used to identify the file when it is subsequently accessed. The file name appears only in the OPEN, CREATE, or FILE statement. The file name and the assigned file number may both be variables. Thus the OPEN statement illustrated above could be replaced by:

```
        FILENAME$ = "PAYROLL.NEW"
        FILENO% = 3
100   OPEN "B:" + FILENAME$   AS FILENO%
```

The CBASIC statement to create the file B:PAYROLL.NEW would be:

```
100   CREATE "B:PAYROLL.NEW"   AS 3
```

This CREATE statement creates a new sequential file on drive B, gives it the name PAYROLL.NEW, and assigns it the number 3 for subsequent file accesses. Note carefully that the number assigned to a file by an OPEN or CREATE statement is effective only until the file is closed. This may be illustrated as follows:

```
100   OPEN "B:PAYROLL.NEW"   AS 3
        -
        -
        -
        -
        All file access statements identify the "PAYROLL"
        file by referencing its number, which is
        currently 3
        -
        -
        -
        CLOSE 3
```

The very next time the PAYROLL.NEW file is opened, it can be assigned a completely different file number.

Every file must have its own unique file number while it is open. This number must be an integer between 1 and 20 inclusive. Up to 20 files may be open at one time.

When a relative file is opened, the fixed record length must be specified using the additional RECL parameter. For example, a mailing list file named MAIL.CAL with 128-byte records is opened on drive A by the following OPEN statement:

```
200   OPEN "A:MAIL.CAL"   RECL 128   AS 9
```

This statement assigns the number 9 to relative MAIL.CAL for subsequent file accesses. Here is the equivalent CREATE statement:

```
200   CREATE "A:MAIL.CAL"   RECL 128   AS 9
```

This CREATE statement would appear once when the MAIL.CAL file was first created. Subsequently, the MAIL.CAL file would be opened using OPEN statements.

CBASIC normally assigns 128-byte buffers to sequential and relative data files when they are opened. Both the OPEN and the CREATE statements allow you to set up data buffers longer than 128 bytes for data files. The BUFF and RECS parameters are used to do this. The BUFF parameter specifies the size of the data buffer for the file being opened or created. The RECS parameter specifies the sector length. (Currently the RECS parameter must be 128.) Sequential file MAIL.SEQ could be opened on drive A with a four-sector data buffer using the following statement:

```
200   OPEN "A:MAIL.SEQ"   AS 9   BUFF 4   RECS 128
```

Provided you have available memory space, opening a sequential file with a multi-sector memory buffer will speed up your program execution time, since the number of diskette accesses are reduced. Suppose, for example, that each record of a file is 50 bytes. A one-sector memory buffer (128 bytes) holds two whole records and part of a third. Therefore, a diskette access will occur every third time a record is read or written. If, on the other hand, a four-sector data buffer (512 bytes) is specified in the OPEN statement, then approximately ten records can be held in this space; therefore diskette accesses will occur with every ten records read or written.

Several files may be specified by a single OPEN or CREATE statement. The following OPEN statement opens a sequential file named PAYROLL.SEQ and a relative file named MAIL.CAL. Both files are opened on drive B:

```
250   OPEN   "B:PAYROLL.SEQ"   AS 3,\
             "B:MAIL.CAL"   RECL 128   AS 9
```

The FILE Statement

The FILE statement will open a file or create it if the file does not already exist. The named file is automatically assigned the lowest available file number. No parameter equivalent to the OPEN and CREATE statements' AS parameter is needed. For relative files the record length must appear after the file name, enclosed in parentheses. Here are some examples:

```
       REM PAYROLL.NEW is a sequential file on drive B
100    FILE "B:PAYROLL.NEW" REM PAYROLL is assigned access no 1.
       REM MAIL.CAL is a relative file on drive C
       REM Records are 128 bytes long
200    FILE "C:MAIL.CAL" (128)   REM MAIL is assigned access no 2.
       REM MAILIST.USA is a relative file on Drive A
       FILENAME$=  "A:MAILIST.USA"
300    FILE   FILENAME$ (128)
```

A single FILE statement can open two or more files. Here is an example:

```
       FILENAME$ = "A:MAILIST.USA"
100    FILE "B:PAYROLL.NEW" , "C:MAIL.CAL" (128),\
            FILENAME$(128)
```

Closing Files

The CLOSE, CHAIN or STOP statements close files. We described the theory behind file closure earlier in this chapter.

The CLOSE Statement

The CLOSE statement closes one or more files. Files to be closed are identified by their access numbers. Here are some examples:

```
100     CREATE   "B:PAYROLL.NEW"   AS 3
        -
        -
        -
5000    CLOSE    3
200     OPEN     "C:MAIL.CAL"   RECL 128   AS 9
        -
        -
        -
4000    CLOSE    9
100     OPEN     "B:MAIL.SEQ"   AS 9   BUFF 4   RECS 128
110     OPEN     "B:PAYROLL.NEW"   AS  3\
                 "C:MAILIST.USA"   RECL(128)   AS 10
        -
        -
        -
2000    CLOSE    9, 3, 10
```

The CHAIN Statement

When the CHAIN statement executes, CBASIC closes any files which were left open in the calling program before fetching the next program. This is especially helpful if you have a series of programs which are connected together as overlays.

The STOP Statement

The STOP statement, when executed, closes all open files. However, it also terminates program execution. STOP is not a substitute for the CLOSE statements, rather CBASIC forces CLOSE operations when STOP is executed, since it is imperative that all files be closed when program execution ceases.

ACCESSING OPEN FILES

You write to open files using the PRINT # and PRINT USING # statements with an additional file identification parameter. You read from an open file using the READ statement.

PRINT # and PRINT USING # Statements with Files

In this chapter we will not fully describe the syntax of the PRINT or PRINT USING statements. The PRINT statement was described in Chapter 4, while the PRINT USING statement was described in Chapter 10. When you write to diskette files using either of these two statements, you must specify the file number as follows:

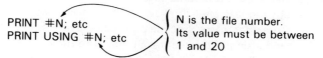

```
PRINT #N; etc              N is the file number.
PRINT USING #N; etc        Its value must be between
                           1 and 20
```

The file number may be any integer or numeric expression that evaluates to a number between 1 and 20. Here is an illustration of PRINT and PRINT USING statements accessing file PAYROLL.NEW on drive B:

```
100   OPEN "B:PAYROLL.NEW"  AS  3
      -
      -
      PRINT #3; etc.
      PRINT USING FORMAT$; #3; etc
      -
      -
      CLOSE  3
```

The file is assigned the access number 3.

When you write data to a diskette file using the PRINT or PRINT USING statement, CBASIC writes the data field by field, exactly as it appears in the PRINT or PRINT USING statement parameter list. PRINT # and PRINT USING # require that every item in the parameter list be separated by a comma. The PRINT # statement will not tabulate when it encounters commas; rather, it prints commas separating each data item. CBASIC does this to make it possible to distinguish between data items when it performs a READ # statement. The commas function as data separators, also called *delimiters*.

Unlike the PRINT and PRINT USING statements which output data to the printer or display, PRINT # and PRINT USING # *cannot* have a delimiter at the end of the parameter list. Remember that this delimiter is used to keep data printing on the same line. All statements which output data to the disk should just end with RETURN.

Calculating Record Lengths

If you use relative data files, you must minimize wasted space. Data file record lengths are not hard to calculate, but calculating the size needed for a record with many fields can be involved. Whenever CBASIC writes a record to any data file, it ends the record with the carriage return and linefeed characters (ASCII codes 0D and 0A hexadecimal). Always allow for two bytes at the end of every record. These are called *record delimiters,* because they serve as an "end of record" signal.

When writing a record with more than one field, CBASIC separates each field with a comma. Commas have special significance as *field delimiters* which signal the end of a field. CBASIC will not write commas if only one data item is written, nor will it write a comma after the last data item. Count one byte per each field (except the last one) to allow for field delimiters.

Quote characters precede and follow every string field. Always add two bytes for each string in the record. Strings, like other data, use the comma as the field delimiter. The quotes distinguish the data item as a string to CBASIC.

For every field there must be a maximum length. Obviously, a string 220 bytes long will not fit into an 80-byte record. For instance, if you had to put together a relative file which would contain information for a check writer program, you would calculate the record length as follows:

Record Contents	Maximum	No. of Bytes Data Delimiters	
Check number	999999	6	+ 1
Date	123199	6	+ 1
Amount	±9999999.99	11	+ 1
Discount percent	99.99	5	+ 1
Discount amount	±9999999.99	11	+ 1
Description	AAAAAAAAAA	10	+ 2
		49 + 7	=56

For record delimiter, add 2 bytes: 58

If you use PRINT USING # to output data to the disk, the record lengths are easier to calculate. Data written to the disk is sent as one string; therefore, by adding two bytes to the string, plus two for the record delimiter, you calculate the record length. The data written in a PRINT USING # statement cannot, however, exceed 255 bytes.

The READ # Statement

The READ # statement fetches data from the disk; it is identified by the key word READ#. This key word is followed by the file number. When reading from relative files the file number is followed by the record number. Variable names complete the READ # statement parameter list. This may be illustrated as follows:

```
REM    Read from sequential file number N%
READ  #N%; variable list
REM    Read from record number RECORD% of
REM    relative file number M%
READ  #M%, RECORD%; variable list
```

Variables in the READ # statement parameter list have values assigned to them sequentially from the identified diskette data record. Consider the example in Figure 11-3. We have deliberately used DATA and READ statements when assigning values to variables in the illustration. The sequential method of assigning values from the DATA statement to variables in the READ statement is identical to the logic used when assigning data from diskette records to variables in a READ # statement. The program changes the number assigned to file DEMO.SEQ when it is opened for a second time to reinforce the fact that this number is an arbitrary program selection.

The program closes file DEMO.SEQ after writing to it; this causes diskette activity to separate the write and subsequent read operation. Since less than 128 bytes of data are written by the PRINT # 1 statement on line 200, no records are written to the diskette until the CLOSE statement is executed. Without closing file DEMO.SEQ and reopening it, therefore, the illustrated program would not demonstrate diskette file accesses at all. The READ # statement on line 300 would read data out of file DEMO.SEQ's buffer, without this data ever having been written to a diskette file.

Notice that the order in which variables are displayed differs from the sequence in which they were generated and written to the diskette. The READ # 2 statement parameter list has variable names that differ from the PRINT # 1 statement parameter list, but variable types are identical. The READ # 2 statement parameter list has a string variable type wherever a string variable was written out to the diskette file. Integer and real variable types also correspond. If you have been reading this book from the beginning, you should be able to correctly guess what happens when the READ # statement variable types do not correspond with the diskette

```
REM       ******DISKETTE FILE ACCESSING DEMO******\
          Write a number of variables to sequential\
          data file DEMO.SEQ.  Read the variables  \
          back in and display them.  MAM 5/1/81     \
          ******************************************

DATA "NUMBERS", 20, 2.7356, "AND", -27.834, 1
REM  Assign data to variables
READ STRING1$, INT1%, REAL1, STRING2$, REAL2, INT2%

REM Create the data file
CREATE "DEMO.SEQ" AS 1
REM Write one record
PRINT #1; STRING1$, INT1%, REAL1, STRING2$, REAL2, INT2%

REM Close the file
CLOSE 1

REM Re-open DEMO.SEQ; read the file and display data read in.
OPEN "DEMO.SEQ" AS 2
READ #2; FIRST.STRING$, FIRST.INT%, FIRST.REAL,\
         SECOND.STRING$, SECOND.REAL, SECOND.INT%

PRINT FIRST.STRING$, FIRST.INT%, FIRST.REAL,\
      SECOND.STRING$, SECOND.REAL, SECOND.INT%

CLOSE 2
STOP
```

Figure 11-3. Writing to and Reading from a Sequential File

record's data types. Conversions are made and errors are reported as they would be anywhere else in a CBASIC program. To recap, this is what happens:

1. Real or integer numeric data can be assigned to a string variable. The number is simply converted to its string equivalent.

2. A real number can be assigned to an integer variable, in which case the real number is truncated.

3. An integer number can be assigned to a real variable, in which case the integer is converted to its real numeric equivalent.

4. A string data item cannot be assigned to any numeric variable. An attempt to do so will result in a run time error.

As an exercise, prove these relationships by changing variable types in the READ #2 statement parameter list on line 300.

OTHER DISK STATEMENTS AND FUNCTIONS

The DELETE Statement

You will frequently need to delete diskette data files. For example, when a program uses temporary diskette files to store transient data, the files should be deleted when the program is done with them. Otherwise your diskette will quickly fill up with junk files that are never accessed.

You remove files from a diskette using the DELETE statement. Files to be deleted are identified by the number assigned in the OPEN statement. A single DELETE statement can delete one or more files. The following statement deletes two files:

```
REM    Files SCRATCH.$$$ and TEMP.$$$
REM    are to be deleted.
OPEN   "B:SCRATCH.$$$" AS 1,\
    "B:TEMP.$$$" AS 2
DELETE  1,2
STOP
```

CBASIC "tells" CP/M to delete the file and to release the file's diskette space. Once deleted, a file is removed from the diskette directory.

The INITIALIZE Statement

Some programs may require the operator to change disks. If you write such a program, the INITIALIZE statement prepares the computer for the disk change. INITIALIZE has no parameters; when CBASIC executes this statement, each diskette should already be changed. If an operator changes diskettes without the INITIALIZE statement, it is possible that the new diskettes will be corrupted; that is, their directories will effectively be ruined.

You must close any open data files before executing an INITIALIZE statement. Here is an example of the INITIALIZE statement in use:

```
100     PRINT "INSERT INVENTORY DISK; <RETURN> WHEN READY"
        WHILE NOT CONSTAT%          REM WAIT FOR CORRECT KEY
        WEND
        IF CONCHAR%< >13 THEN 100   REM ONLY ACCEPT RETURN
        INITIALIZE                  REM SET UP NEW DISK
        IF END #1 THEN 100          REM DON'T ALLOW WRONG DISK
        OPEN "INVFILE.DTA" RECL 1024 AS 1
          -
          -
          -
          -
```

The RENAME Function

The RENAME function changes a file's name. Being a function, RENAME must be used as a variable in a CBASIC statement. This function has two string arguments: the first is the new file name; the second is the file to rename. The file to rename cannot be an open file. The new file name cannot already exist on the diskette. A value of −1 returns if the diskette file is successfully renamed. A value of 0 is returned if, for any reason, the diskette file cannot be renamed. Here is a programming example:

```
REM   Change file OLDNAME.REL to NEWNAME.REL
DUMMY% = RENAME ("NEWNAME.REL", "OLDNAME.REL", "OLDNAME.REL")
```

Or we could use:

```
NEW$ = "NEWNAME. REL"
OLD$ = "OLDNAME.REL"
DUMMY% = RENAME (NEW$, OLD$)
```

Although the example shown above would work, it does not represent good programming practice. Since RENAME tells you whether the operation was or was not successful, use it in a conditional statement as follows:

```
IF NOT RENAME (NEW$, OLD$) THEN 10000
    -
    -
    -
    -
10000   REM Diskette rename error recovery routine
```

The SIZE Function

This function returns the size of the file, expressed in 1024-byte increments. You can determine the size of one file, a group of files or all files on the diskette. This function is not highly accurate, but it is very useful if your program is to check for available space on a diskette before continuing.

The SIZE function is denoted by the key word SIZE followed by a file name parameter in parentheses. The file name parameter can be *ambiguous;* that is, it can refer to more than one file on the diskette. An ambiguous file name uses question mark and asterisk characters to describe unspecified portions of a name. The question mark represents a single unspecified character; the asterisk represents an unspecified file name and/or file suffix. The unspecified portion of an ambiguous file name is thought of as a "wild card," where any character or set of characters would be acceptable.

To illustrate ambiguous file names, consider the SIZE function:

```
A% = SIZE("AB?C.BAS")
```

The ? character in this ambiguous file name is not compared. Therefore any of the following file names would be selected; their file sizes would be added together and returned in the SIZE function:

AB1C.BAS
ABZC.BAS
ABXC.BAS

Here is another ambiguous file name:

A???.BAS

Any file name will be selected providing the primary name has four characters, the first of which is an A, while the suffix is .BAS.

The asterisk character used in ambiguous file names may be illustrated as follows:

ABCD.*

The sizes of all files named ABCD with any suffix will be returned.
Similarly the ambiguous file name:

*.BAS

will return the total size of files with the suffix .BAS.
The ambiguous file name:

.

will return *all* disk space used by all files, since an asterisk in the file name and its suffix will select any and every file on the diskette. On the other hand, the ambiguous file name:

????.???

will select any file with a four-character file name having a three-character suffix.

SIZE will not work accurately if the file is already open and you have been appending data to it. CP/M actually passes the file size statistic to CBASIC, and you have to update the diskette directory to get a correct SIZE answer. Therefore, close a file before getting its SIZE.

FILE HANDLING PROGRAM EXAMPLES

Next we will write some simple programs to demonstrate the difference between sequential files and relative files. These programs will store 15 records on a diskette file; the two fields within the record will be the string "RECORD NUMBER", followed by the number of the record.

The program in Figure 11-4 creates a sequential file and stores records in it. The program in Figure 11-5 reads records from the sequential file SEQ.DTA, displaying each record as it is read. The programs in Figures 11-4 and 11-5 are

```
REM   CREATE A SEQUENTIAL DATA FILE
CREATE "SEQ.DTA" AS 1

REM   WRITE 15 RECORDS
FOR I% = 1 TO 15
    PRINT #1; "RECORD NUMBER", I%
NEXT I%

CLOSE 1
STOP
```

Figure 11-4. Writing 15 Records to a Sequential File,
using the CREATE Statement

```
REM   OPEN SEQUENTIAL FILE SEQ.DTA,
REM   READ ITS CONTENTS AND DISPLAY EACH RECORD

OPEN "SEQ.DTA" AS 1
FOR I% = 1 TO 15
    READ #1; STRING$, NUM%
    PRINT STRING$, NUM%
NEXT I%
CLOSE 1
STOP
```

Figure 11-5. Reading 15 Records from the File SEQ.DTA

easily changed to access relative files. A 13-byte string ("RECORD NUMBER")
and an integer with a maximum length of two digits will be written; a comma separates the second field from the first; adding two bytes to the record length to
allow for a carriage return/line feed pair at the end of the record, the total record
length would be 18 bytes. We will use a record length of 20 bytes for the relative
file. The CREATE statement changes as shown in Figure 11-6. The OPEN statement will not change because the file will still be read sequentially. However, random access is not possible if an OPEN statement does not specify a record length,
even if the file was created with fixed-length records.

The file name change from SEQ.DTA to REL.DTA is for cosmetic purposes
only. The name change has no programming significance whatsoever. To demonstrate the random-access features of relative files, the program in Figure 11-7
reads file REL.DTA backwards, from the 15th to the first record. The record number expression, (16-I%), decrements to read each previous record.

```
REM   CREATE A RELATIVE DATA FILE
CREATE "REL.DTA" RECL 20 AS 1

REM   WRITE 15 RECORDS
FOR I% = 1 TO 15
    PRINT #1; "RECORD NUMBER", I%
NEXT I%
CLOSE 1
STOP
```

Figure 11-6. Writing 15 Records to a Relative File

```
REM   OPEN RELATIVE FILE REL.DTA
REM   READ ITS CONTENTS BACKWARDS AND DISPLAY EACH RECORD

OPEN "REL.DTA" RECL 20 AS 1
FOR I% = 1 TO 15
    READ #1, (16 - I%); STRING$,NUM%
    PRINT STRING$, NUM%
NEXT I%
CLOSE 1
STOP
```

Figure 11-7. Reading a Relative File Backwards

The IF END # Statement

We have written programs that read records from sequential or relative files assuming that the number of records in the file is known. What if the number of records in the file is unknown? You should then use an IF END # statement. The IF END # statement, identified by the key words IF END #, causes program logic to branch when a file access error occurs. Using the IF END # statement, the program in Figure 11-5 could be rewritten as follows:

```
REM Open Sequential file SEQ.DTA.  \
    Read and display records until \
    end of file condition exists.

IF END #1 THEN 300                      REM Set error branch

OPEN "SEQ.DTA" AS 1

250 READ #1; STRING$, NUMBER%           REM Read a record
    PRINT STRING$, NUMBER%              REM Display it
    GOTO 250

300 PRINT "END OF FILE"
    STOP
```

In the example above, the IF END # statement will cause a branch if the READ # statement executed for a file which has already been fully read and contains no more data. This is called an *end of file* condition. The IF END # statement can also be used to detect nonexistent files. An IF END # statement preceding an OPEN statement will cause a branch if the OPEN statement refers to a nonexistent file. This may be illustrated as follows:

```
IF END # 3 THEN 10000
OPEN FILE$ AS 3
```

If the file named by FILE$ does not exist then a branch to statement 10000 will occur. Each IF END # statement is connected to an OPEN or READ # statement by the file number, as illustrated above. For example, the IF END # statement specifying file 3 is connected to the following OPEN statement, which opens FILE$ as file 3.

The IF END # statement is unusual because its effect covers the next OPEN or READ # statement specifying the same file number. It is the OPEN or READ # statement that triggers the IF END # program branch. An OPEN statement triggers the IF END # program branch on attempting to open a nonexistent file. A READ # statement triggers the IF END # program branch on detecting an end of file.

Two or more IF END # statements can be present, each connected to one subsequent OPEN or READ # statements by a file number. This may be illustrated as follows:

```
100   IF END #1 THEN 10000
      OPEN FILE1$ AS 1
200   IF END #2 THEN 1000.1
      OPEN FILE2$ AS 2
300   IF END #3 THEN 10000.2
        -
        -
        -
        -
400   READ #3; etc.
        -
        -
        -
        -
```

The IF END O statement on line 100 is connected to the OPEN statement for FILE1$. The IF END O statement on line 200, likewise, is connected to the OPEN for FILE2$, and so on. The READ O statement on line 400 will cause a branch to line 1000.2 if an end of file condition exists.

Always use IF END # statements with OPEN statements. If the computer operator puts the wrong diskette in a drive, then in all probability the executing program will not find the data file it is looking for on this diskette. In the absence of an IF END # statement a disk access error would occur, the operator would receive an obscure error message, and program execution would cease. The IF

END # statement could branch to an error recovery routine that tells the operator to check the data diskette, then press some appropriate key to continue program execution.

APPENDING DATA TO SEQUENTIAL FILES

The IF END statement can be used to write additional data at the end of a sequential file. Here are the necessary steps:

1. Execute and IF END # statement for the file to open.
2. Open the sequential file.
3. Read the file; repeat until the end of the file is reached.
4. Write new data to the end of the sequential file.
5. Close the file.

The program in Figure 11-8 starts writing new data records to the end of file SEQ.DTA, which was created by the program in Figure 11-4. Figure 11-9 writes two additional records to the end of relative file REL.DTA. This file was created by the program in Figure 11-6.

We specify a user-defined function to compute the first record number in the last 1024-byte block of the relative file since a real program would be likely to make this calculation many times. Note that the SIZE function is used to compute the file size. This function returns the number of 1024-byte blocks currently assigned a file. This function, when divided by the record length, returns the number of records in the file up until the last 1024-byte block. Here, string variable FILE.NAME$ identifies the file.

The special user function FN.LAST.REC% is used to identify the last record of file REL.DTA. The IF END statement is then used to identify the actual end of file, while fields are read one by one using the READ #1 statement on line 100. When the end of file is detected the prior IF-END statement causes a branch to line 200, where the statement sequence to write two more records begins.

CBASIC DATA FILE CONVENTIONS

Data file update modules are common programs you will have to write. If you follow good programming practice, you will always maintain two versions of an updated file: the current version and a backup version. The backup is the version prior to the most recent set of changes. If you follow CBASIC conventions, then the backup file should have the secondary name BAK.

```
              REM   ADD TWO NEW RECORDS TO FILE SEQ.DTA

              REM   IF FILE SEQ.DTA IS NOT FOUND,
              REM   BRANCH TO STATEMENT 10000
              IF END #1 THEN 10000

              OPEN "SEQ.DTA" AS 1

              REM   FIND THE END OF FILE #1
              IF END #1 THEN 300
   200          READ #1; STRING$, NUM%
                GOTO 200

              REM   WRITE TWO ADDITIONAL RECORDS
   300        FOR I% = 1 TO 2
                PRINT #1; STRING$, NUM% + I%
              NEXT I%

  10000       REM   ERROR CODE FOR "FILE NOT FOUND" BEGINS HERE

              CLOSE 1
              STOP
```

Figure 11-8. A Program which Appends Data to the
End of an Existing File

```
              REM   FN.LAST.BLK% FINDS THE NUMBER OF THE FIRST RECORD
              REM   OF THE LAST BLOCK OCCUPPIED BY A RELATIVE FILE

              DEF   FN.LAST.BLK% (FILE.NAME$,REC.SIZE%)
                    FILE.SIZE% = SIZE(FILE.NAME$)
                    FN.LAST.BLK% = ((FILE.SIZE% - 1) * 1024)/ REC.SIZE% + 1
                    RETURN
              FEND


              REM   ADD TWO RECORDS TO THE END OF FILE REL.DTA

              IF END #1 THEN 10000     REM   ERROR - FILE NOT FOUND
              OPEN "REL.DTA" RECL 25 AS 1

              REM   FIND END OF FILE BY READING ALL RECORDS IN LAST BLOCK
              IF END #1 THEN 200
                READ #1,FN.LAST.BLK%("REL.DTA",20);STRING$, NUM%
   100          READ #1; STRING$, NUM%
                GOTO 100

   200        REM   END OF FILE DETECTED.  WRITE TWO RECORDS
              FOR I% = 1 TO 2
                PRINT #1; STRING$, NUM% + I%
              NEXT I%

  10000       REM   ERROR CODE FOR FILE NOT FOUND BEGINS HERE

              CLOSE 1
              STOP
```

Figure 11-9. Appending Data to a Diskette File, with User-defined
Function to find the End of Any File

These are the actual steps you should follow when updating a file:

1. Create a temporary file. Following CBASIC conventions this file will have the suffix $$$.
2. Update the current file, storing the updated version in the temporary file.
3. When the file has been updated, close the temporary file and the "old" current file.
4. Delete the "old" backup file.
5. Rename the old current file, making it the new backup file.
6. Rename the temporary file, making it the new current file.

A MAILING LIST FILE HANDLING PROGRAM

We will now describe complete file handling program logic using the mailing list program as the basis for our example. These are the required program steps:

1. Create and open files.
2. Create new mailing list records using the program described in Figure 9-1.
3. Write new records into a temporary file.
4. Let the operator identify current old records that need to be modified or deleted.
5. Copy old records to the temporary file, allowing the operator to modify selected records.
6. Delete the backup file.
7. Rename the current file to become the new backup file.
8. Rename the temporary file to become the new current file.

If you are a beginning programmer, it is very important that you write this complete program and make sure it is working correctly. We will explain changes and additions you must make to the program illustrated in Figure 9-1, but we will not create a complete executable program.

For Step 1 we use a single FILE statement:

```
REM   Open files at the beginning of the program.
FILE   "MAILIST.$$$" (128), \Scratch file, #1
       "MAILIST.CUR" (128), \ Current file, #2
       "MAILIST.BAK" (128) \ Backup file, #3
```

This is a good place to use the FILE statement since a new file has to be created while old files need to opened. This FILE statement should appear near the beginning of the program, somewhere ahead of statements that create name and address records.

You can use the program illustrated in Figure 9-1 for Step 2. We will keep statements beginning at line 1200. These statements concatenate the name and address into a single string variable to check for a record that is too long. But the STOP statement below line 1200 must be removed and statements added writing the name and address record to temporary file MAILIST.$$$. Here are the necessary statements:

```
        IF LEN(NAD$) > 128 THEN GOTO 10010
        REM Write a valid name and address to the scratch file
        PRINT #1; NAME$, STREET$, CITY$, STATE$, ZIP$
        REM Ask if additional data is to be entered.
1300    INPUT "CONTINUE? ENTER Y OR N" ; Y$
        IF Y$ = "Y" THEN GOTO 1000   REM Enter another record
        IF Y$ < > "N" THEN GOTO 1300   REM Invalid response
        REM When operator enters N to end,
        REM verify the response
1400    INPUT "ARE YOU SURE? ENTER Y OR N" ; Y$
        IF Y$ < > "Y" THEN GOTO 1300
        REM Start post processing
```

We have added some routine dialogue that allows the operator to enter another name and address, or continue to Step 3 of the program where post-processing begins. Post-processing covers Steps 4 through 8. We will not write the program for Steps 4 and 5 since there are innumerable ways in which these steps could be programmed.

You could ask the operator to enter the name field for name and address records that must be modified or deleted. Most computers will have sufficient memory to store a large number of name fields. This information should be held in memory, in a one-dimensional array.

Next, read records sequentially from file MAILIST.CUR. Compare the NAME$ field with the vector identifying records to be changed. If there is no match, write the record to file IMALIST.$$$. If the record is to be deleted, do not write it to file MAILIST.$$$ and the record is deleted. If the record is to be changed, make appropriate changes using program logic found in Figure 9-1 beginning at line 1010. After all changes have been made, write the record to file MAILIST.$$$.

After all records from file MAILIST.CUR have been processed, we can proceed to Steps 6, 7, and 8. Here are the necessary statements:

```
        REM   Update mailing list files
        DELETE 3
        IF NOT RENAME ("MAILIST.BAK" , "MAILIST.CUR") \
          THEN 10020
        IF NOT RENAME ("MAILIST.CUR" , "MAILIST.$$$") \
          THEN 10030
        CLOSE 1,2
        STOP
```

You now need to add appropriate error recovery logic at lines 10000, 10010, 10020, and 10030 and the program is complete.

12
CBASIC Runtime Organization

THIS CHAPTER WILL DISCUSS the organization of memory during execution of a CBASIC program. The format used to store each type of variable, the effect of chaining on the memory organization, and the method of interfacing with the operating system will be covered. Knowledge of this chapter is not required to use CBASIC; it is included to provide insight for the advanced programmer.

The CBASIC compiler translates source statements into instructions for a hypothetical computer which we will call the CBASIC computer. The runtime monitor, CRUN2, simulates this computer by executing each of the instructions generated by the compiler. The CBASIC computer is a stack-oriented computer much like a Hewlett Packard calculator. It provides a friendly environment for execution of CBASIC programs on the 8080 or Z80 microprocessor. The discussion that follows assumes an understanding of the CP/M operating system.

THE STRUCTURE OF MEMORY AT RUNTIME

A CBASIC program is executed by entering the command CRUN2 followed by the name of the program to be executed. CP/M loads the runtime monitor into the *transient program area* (TPA) and then begins executing it. The memory available in the TPA is partitioned into six areas of variable size. Figure 12-1 illustrates this memory organization. The first partition contains the *runtime monitor*. The remaining five areas are used by the runtime monitor during execution of a program.

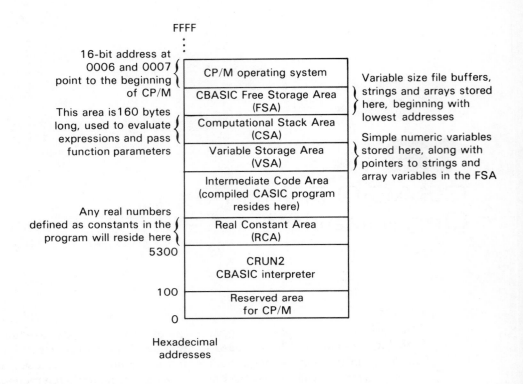

FFFF

16-bit address at 0006 and 0007 point to the beginning of CP/M

This area is 160 bytes long, used to evaluate expressions and pass function parameters

CP/M operating system	
CBASIC Free Storage Area (FSA)	
Computational Stack Area (CSA)	
Variable Storage Area (VSA)	
Intermediate Code Area (compiled CASIC program resides here)	
Real Constant Area (RCA)	
CRUN2 CBASIC interpreter	
Reserved area for CP/M	

Variable size file buffers, strings and arrays stored here, beginning with lowest addresses

Simple numeric variables stored here, along with pointers to strings and array variables in the FSA

Any real numbers defined as constants in the program will reside here

5300

100

0

Hexadecimal addresses

Figure 12-1. CBASIC Run-time Memory Map

The first partition is the *real constant area* (RCA). It is used to store all real numbers that are defined as constants in the program. A real constant requires eight bytes of storage. If the same constant is used more than once in the program it appears only once in the RCA. The real constant 1.0 is always the first constant stored, even if it is not used by the program. Thus the real constant partition will always be at least eight bytes in length.

Following the list of real constants a partition is reserved to store the intermediate code. This is where instructions are stored for the CBASIC computer. When the program is executed, instructions are fetched from the *intermediate code area* (ICA) and action required by each instruction is executed.

The *variable storage area* (VSA) contains space to store the current value of each variable used by the program. Eight bytes of storage are reserved for each variable, regardless of the variable type. If a program has 10 variables, 80 bytes of memory are reserved. The first variable encountered in the program is stored in the first eight bytes of the VSA, the second in the next eight bytes, etc. Since

COMMON statements must be the first statements in a program, common variables appear first in the VSA. There is no COMMON area as such. The beginning of the VSA contains all the variables which are assigned to COMMON.

The VSA is the permanent storage location for each variable. If the variable is an array or if it is a string (or both) the actual "value" of the variable is located in the free storage area (FSA) described below. In this case the value stored in the VSA will be the location of the actual variable in the FSA. The reason for this is that strings and arrays are dynamic structures that are created and released during program execution. This will be discussed in more detail shortly. Initially, numeric variables are set to zero and string variables are set to null strings. If the value in the VSA for a string variable is 0 the string is treated as a null string. Likewise, a value of 0 for an array variable indicates the array has not been dimensioned.

The *computation stack area* (CSA) occupies the next 160 bytes of memory. This allows for 20 eight-byte real numbers to be placed on the stack. The stack is implemented by software and has no relation to the hardware stack of the microprocessor. Stack overflow or underflow is not detected. If the stack overflows it overwrites the free storage area, described next.

The computation stack is used to evaluate expressions and to pass parameters to user defined or predefined functions. Subroutine calls use a different stack within the runtime monitor for return addresses.

The remaining TPA area is used as a *free storage area* (FSA). This is a generally available area within which variably-sized blocks of memory may be allocated as required. When a particular block of memory is no longer needed it is returned to the free storage area for reuse. It is in the free storage area that strings and arrays are stored. In addition, buffers for files are allocated in the free storage area as required.

The six areas described above make up the structure of the CBASIC computer. The size of each area is fixed when the runtime monitor is executed and remains static during the entire time the program is executed. With the exception of the stack, the size of each of these areas is encoded into the intermediate file produced by the compiler. Thus the location of the areas varies from one program to another.

FORMAT OF VARIABLES

CBASIC supports real and integer numeric variables as well as string variables. Integer numbers are stored as 16-bit 2's complement binary numbers, low-order byte first. This format was selected because microprocessors can operate directly on these numbers. Figure 12-2 gives examples of the format used to store integers.

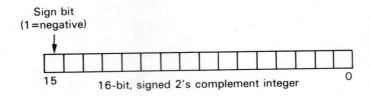

Sign bit
(1 =negative)

15   16-bit, signed 2's complement integer   0

Decimal Number	CBASIC Internal Representation	
	Low-Order Byte	High-Order Byte
1	0000 0001	0000 0000
32767	1111 1111	0111 1111
−1	1111 1111	1111 1111
5	0000 0101	0000 0000

Figure 12-2. Internal Representation of CBASIC Integers

Real numbers are stored as eight-byte binary coded decimal (BCD) floating-point numbers. As shown in Figure 12-3, the first byte contains the sign of the number and a seven-bit decimal exponent. The remaining seven bytes make up the mantissa. Each byte of the mantissa contains two BCD digits. The mantissa is always stored in a normalized form so that the decimal point is assumed to be to the left of the most significant digit. In each byte, the digit represented by the first four bits is more significant than the last four bits, which represent the next digit. The byte farthest from the exponent contains the most significant digits in the number. Figure 12-4 gives examples of real numbers.

Strings are stored as a sequential list of characters preceded by the string length. Figure 12-5 shows the format used for strings.

Since one byte is allowed for string length, the maximum number of characters in a string is 255. For instance, the string "Hi there" would be stored as nine consecutive bytes of memory. The first byte would be a binary 8, the length of the string. The remaining eight bytes hold the ASCII characters H, i, etc.

Strings created during execution of a program are stored in the free storage area. String constants which are defined in the source program are stored in the intermediate code partition.

Both numeric and string arrays are stored in the free storage area. When a DIM statement is executed, sufficient space is allocated in the free storage area for the entire array. If the array contains real numbers, eight bytes are reserved for each element of the array. Two bytes are reserved for integer arrays and three bytes are reserved per entry for string arrays. In addition to the space reserved for the elements of the array, space is reserved to allow the location of a specific element to

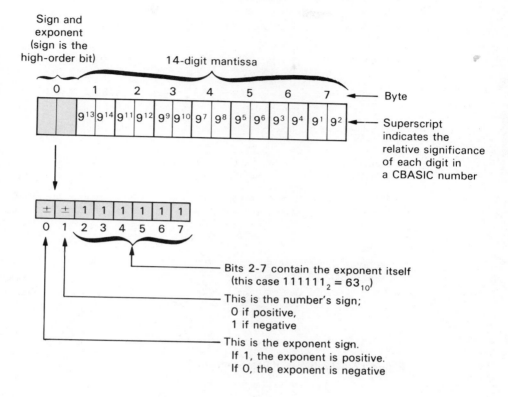

Figure 12-3. Internal Representation of CBASIC Real Numbers

be calculated. Figure 12-6 shows the space required for a two-dimensional array. This information precedes the actual array elements and is referred to as a *dope vector*. The dope vector contains one byte plus two additional bytes for each dimension in the array. For instance, DIM X(12,10) would reserve five bytes for the dope vector and 1144 bytes for the elements of the array, for a total of 1149 bytes of storage.

Real Number   BCD equivalent (hexadecimal notation)

3.14159   41   00   00   00   04   59   41   31
                                                          ⌃
                                                          Assumed decimal

               ⌣⌣ LSB   ••   ••   ••   MSB-2 MSB-1 MSB
               exponent

700   4 3   0 0   0 0   0 0   0 0   0 0   0 0   7 0
(7E2)   ⌃
                                                              Assumed decimal

               ⌣⌣ LSB   ••   ••   ••   ••   ••   MSB
               exponent

−10000.4   C 5   0 0   0 0   0 0   0 0   0 4   0 0   1 0
(−1,00004 E4)   ⌃
                                                              Assumed decimal

               ⌣⌣ LSB   ••   ••   ••   ••   ••   MSB
               exponent

Figure 12-4. Examples of Real Numbers

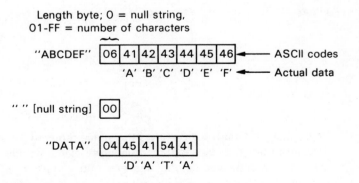

Length byte; 0 = null string,
01-FF = number of characters

"ABCDEF" | 06 | 41 | 42 | 43 | 44 | 45 | 46 | ◄─── ASCII codes
               'A' 'B' 'C' 'D' 'E' 'F' ◄─── Actual data

" " [null string] | 00 |

"DATA" | 04 | 45 | 41 | 54 | 41 |
             'D' 'A' 'T' 'A'

Figure 12-5. Internal Representation of Strings

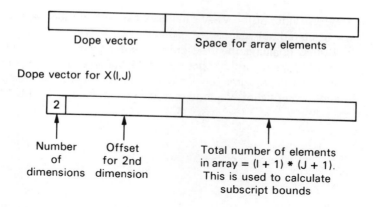

Figure 12-6. Space Required for an Array

INTERFACING WITH CP/M

The CBASIC runtime monitor operates with the CP/M operating system for all communication with the outside world. This includes access to disk files, printers, and the console. Standard CP/M system calls as defined in the Digital Research CP/M documentation are used for all CP/M interfaces.

CBASIC has a number of different configurations to support different versions of CP/M. Configuration 0 of CBASIC will operate with all versions of CP/M and MP/M; however, the maximum size of a random access disk file that is read and written is approximately 250,000 bytes. This would fill one single-density 8-inch diskette. Configuration 3 of the CBASIC runtime monitor is designed to operate with either CP/M version 2 or MP/M. It will not work with CP/M version 1. Configuration 3 uses CP/M system calls available only in CP/M version 2 or MP/M. This enables both sequential and random files to grow to 8 million characters.

Configuration 1 of CBASIC is identical to configuration 0 except that it is designed to operate with CP/M on the TRS-80 model 1.

CHAINING

When a CHAIN statement is executed by the runtime monitor a new intermediate file is read into main memory. The runtime monitor retains the six areas originally established when the program was executed. The new intermediate code is loaded into the ICA, and the new real constants are placed in the RCA. (Refer to Figure 12-1). The variables in the VSA which are also in COMMON remain intact.

The remainder of the VSA is initialized so that numbers are set to zero and strings are assigned null values.

During chaining the free storage area is compacted. All the space is made available except for that space which is occupied by strings or arrays which are in COMMON. If a program chains to itself, the free storage area is cleared of all information except that which is stored in variables in COMMON.

13
The Machine Interface

ALTHOUGH MOST APPLICATIONS can be written in CBASIC without resorting to assembly language, CBASIC provides facilities to control the computer directly using assembly language programs along with CBASIC programs. This chapter describes CBASIC statements which locate variables in memory and pass the contents of memory to and from a CBASIC program. In this chapter you will learn how to implement an assembly language routine and integrate it with a CBASIC program. To use the features described in this chapter, you should have an understanding of assembly language programming and the CP/M operating system.

The POKE Statement

The POKE statement will convert an expression to a one-byte integer and place it at the memory address you specify. For example:

```
POKE 45,100
```

will put the decimal value 100 in address 45. The address and the expression to POKE both have to be integer or real numbers; strings are not allowed. The next example shows how a string could be passed to an assembly language routine. The integer variable ADDRESS% contains the location you begin moving the string to. MSG$ is the string to place in memory.

```
I%=0
WHILE I% < LEN(MSG$)
  POKE ADDRESS%+I%, ASC(MID$(MSG$,I%+1,1))
  I%=I%+1
WEND
```

The PEEK Function

The PEEK function does the opposite of POKE; it fetches a one-byte value equal to the contents of an address you specify in parentheses. For example:

X%=PEEK(80H)

will assign the variable X% with the value stored in memory address 80H (remember, 'H' is used to denote a hexadecimal number; in base 10, this address would be 128). The expression in parentheses can be a real or integer value.

The CALL Statement

The CALL statement transfers control of the computer to an assembly language subroutine from a CBASIC program. Its logic is similar to GOSUB logic; if the subroutine executes an assembly language RET (return) instruction, the computer will resume execution of the CBASIC program with the statement immediately following CALL. The following statement:

CALL 3000

will start execution of an assembly language subroutine starting at address 3000. The subroutine will return to the CBASIC program when it executes an 8080 or Z80 RET instruction (C9 object code). The statement:

CALL ROUTINE.LOC%+ENTRY4%

calls an assembly language subroutine at the location determined by adding the integer variables ROUTINE.LOC% and ENTRY4% together.

The microprocessor's registers may be altered by the machine language subroutine, and, with the exception of the stack-pointer, they need not be restored before returning from the assembly language subroutine. CBASIC will support four additional levels of assembly language subroutine calls. Your subroutine will have to maintain its own stack if more levels are needed.

Locating Variables in Memory —
The SADD and VARPTR Functions

CBASIC provides two functions which return the address of a variable in memory. These functions are vital if you write assembly language subroutines which use CBASIC variables as input.

The SADD function returns a 16-bit signed integer which represents the address of the string variable in parentheses. For example:

I%=SADD(A$)

will set I% to the address of the first byte of string variable A$. The argument within parentheses must be a string variable name. Numeric variables are not permitted. SADD will pass the address of the length byte of the string, which immediately precedes the first character of the string itself. If SADD is used to locate a null string, the function will return an address of zero or it will return a string address which has a length byte set to zero.

To find the location of a numeric variable in memory, use VARPTR. In contrast to SADD, which only works with strings, VARPTR will work with all data types. This function will return the address of a numeric variable as a signed 16-bit integer; however, the VARPTR function used with a string variable will pass a value which points not to the string, but to another signed 16-bit integer which in turn points to the actual string.

CBASIC allocates strings dynamically, and the address of a string's contents can vary while the program executes. The pointers to string variables, however, always remain at the same memory location. Look at the illustrations below to understand the difference between VARPTR results for string and for numeric data items.

```
REM SET VALUES FOR VARIABLES
A$="STRING"
B%=-32767

REM PRINT LOCATION OF INTEGER VARIABLE
PRINT "B% AT ADDRESS";VARPTR(B%)

REM FETCH STRING POINTER FOR A$
POINTER%=VARPTR(A$)

PRINT "A$ POINTER IS AT ADDRESS";POINTER%
PRINT "FIRST BYTE OF A$ IS AT ADDRESS";\
       PEEK(POINTER%+1)*256+PEEK(POINTER%)
```

INTERFACING ASSEMBLY LANGUAGE
ROUTINES WITH CBASIC PROGRAMS

A CBASIC program can automatically load an assembly language program directly into memory from disk using the SAVEMEM statement. Actually, SAVEMEM can load any disk file; this is especially useful if your CBASIC program will load file indexes or other mass amounts of data.

SAVEMEM loads the file into the highest available addresses of the transient program area (TPA). CBASIC will not interfere with this area; instead, the free storage area (see Chapter 12) is reduced in order to accommodate the memory needed for the file read in from disk. If the file contains an assembly language subroutine, your CBASIC program can execute the routine once the SAVEMEM statement has loaded it into memory.

SAVEMEM specifies the name of the file to load into memory and how much memory to reserve for the file. The general form of a SAVEMEM statement is:

SAVEMEM *integer constant, string expression*

where *integer constant* specifies the size of the area to reserve, and *string expression* evaluates to the name of the file to load into memory. The file name string can be a constant, variable or expression, but the integer must be a constant; not a variable or expression. Only one SAVEMEM statement may appear in a program. As an example:

SAVEMEM 256, "INPUT.COM"

will load the file INPUT.COM into memory starting at the location 256 bytes below the highest address in the transient program area. When CBASIC executes this statement, the file will be loaded into memory until it is completely read in, or until loading additional data would cause the area above the TPA to be overwritten.

If the integer constant is less than 128, CBASIC will still set aside the amount of memory specified in the SAVEMEM statement, but no data will be read from the file; similarly, if the file name is a null string, space is reserved but no data is loaded into the reserved area. If a main program and a series of chained programs use SAVEMEM statements, the chained programs will have to set aside the same amount of memory as the first SAVEMEM statement; each program can load a different file, but the amount of memory allocated must be constant from the main program to each one chained.

Creating the Assembly Language Routine

For illustration, we will develop an assembly language subroutine that converts all upper-case alphabetic characters in a string to lower-case. The CBASIC program will pass the memory address of the string to the assembly language routine and then execute the routine. The assembly language routine will convert each upper-case character in the string to lower-case, leaving any other characters in the string unchanged. Enter the program shown in Figure 13-1 on your computer using ED or any other text editor which the CP/M assembler, ASM.COM, will accept.

Assemble the program now that you have entered it. The assembler creates two files from FIG13-1.ASM. FIG13-1.HEX is the assembled program, stored in Intel MDS hexadecimal format. Actually, the program is not yet in object code; the file is the ASCII representation of the assembly language program's object code.

The second file, FIG13-1.PRN, is the assembly language program in both its

```
;
;              ASSEMBLY LANGUAGE ROUTINE TO CONVERT
;              STRING TO LOWER CASE
;
STRING: DW         0

   LCS:      LHLD      STRING    ; LOAD STRING ADDRESS
             MOV       A,H
             ORA       L         ; IF ADDRESS IS ZERO, EXIT
             RZ
             MOV       A,M       ; IF LENGTH BYTE IS ZERO, ALSO EXIT
             ORA       A
             RZ
             MOV       E,A       ; OTHERWISE MOVE LENGTH INTO REG E

   LC1:      INX       H         ; CONVERSION ROUTINE
             MOV       A,M
             SUI       'A'
             CPI       26        ; SKIP CONVERSION IF CHARACTER IS LOWER CASE
             JNC       LC2
             MOV       A,M       ; MOVE CHARACTER TO ACCUMULATOR
             ORI       20H       ; CONVERT IT TO LOWER CASE
             MOV       M,A       ; REPLACE IT IN MEMORY
   LC2:      DCR       E         ; DECREMENT LENGTH COUNTER
             JNZ       LC1       ; IF E>0 THEN CONTINUE
             RET                 ; ELSE RETURN
```

Figure 13-1. ASM with an Assumed Start
Address of 0

```
A>ASM FIG13-1
CP/M ASSEMBLER - VER 1.4
001E ◄─────── Next available address
000H USE FACTOR
END OF ASSEMBLY
```

Figure 13-2. Using ASM.COM to Assemble the Upper-to-Lower
Case Conversion Routine

source code and object code forms, stored in a format which allows you to print the file out. Figure 13-2 shows how FIG13-1.ASM is assembled. Notice that the shaded area toward the bottom of this figure is the last address used by the program assembled. This number, 001E, is 30 decimal; this listing shows that 30 (1EH) bytes are required by the program. This size figure will be needed for SAVEMEM.

Normally, an assembly language program written for CP/M originates at address 256 (100H), at the beginning of the TPA. Most assemblers are informed of a program's starting address by using an origin (ORG) statement. Thus for a typical assembly language program the ORG statement would be:

ORG 100H

When using SAVEMEM, the assembly language program is loaded at the *top* of the TPA. You have to calculate the origin of the program. This is necessary because CBASIC will load the assembly language subroutine at the highest addresses available, and CP/M varies in size from system to system. CP/M stores the address immediately above the TPA at addresses 6 and 7. Address 6 contains the low-order byte of the 16-bit address, followed by the high-order byte at address 7. The following CBASIC statements derive this address:

PRINT "ADDRESS 7 (HIGH-ORDER):"; PEEK(7)
PRINT "ADDRESS 6 (LOW-ORDER):"; PEEK(6)

Converting the results of the two PEEK statements on the system used to develop the assembly language subroutine, the result is 61702 (F106 hexadecimal). Next, take the length of the assembly language program (30 bytes) and round it up to the nearest multiple of 128. The integer constant would be 128 for the SAVEMEM statement in the case of FIG13-1.ASM. SAVEMEM will only read data in from the disk in multiples of 128 bytes. Now subtract 128 from the top of the TPA determined above, which results in a value of 0F086H. This is the origin for the assembly language routine when used with the CBASIC program. Re-edit FIG13-1.ASM, substituting the ORG 0 with the address you calculated. Figure 13-3 shows the program reassembled at the correct origin.

```
                    ;
                    ;        ASSEMBLY LANGUAGE ROUTINE TO CONVERT
                    ;        STRING TO LOWER CASE
                    ;
F086                         ORG      0F086H   ; ORG AT SAVEMEM LOCATION THIS TIME
F086 0000   STRING: DW       0
F088 2A86F0 LCS:    LHLD     STRING   ; LOAD STRING ADDRESS
F08B 7C             MOV      A,H
F08C B5             ORA      L        ; IF ADDRESS IS ZERO, EXIT
F08D C8             RZ
F08E 7E             MOV      A,M      ; IF LENGTH BYTE IS ZERO, ALSO EXIT
F08F B7             ORA      A
F090 C8             RZ
F091 5F             MOV      E,A      ; OTHERWISE MOVE LENGTH INTO REG E
F092 23     LC1:    INX      H        ; CONVERSION ROUTINE
F093 7E             MOV      A,M
F094 D641           SUI      'A'
F096 FE1A           CPI      26       ; SKIP CONVERSION IF CHARACTER IS LOWER CASE
F098 D29FF0         JNC      LC2
F09B 7E             MOV      A,M      ; MOVE CHARACTER TO ACCUMULATOR
F09C F620           ORI      20H      ; CONVERT IT TO LOWER CASE
F09E 77             MOV      M,A      ; REPLACE IT IN MEMORY
F09F 1D     LC2:    DCR      E        ; DECREMENT LENGTH COUNTER
F0A0 C292F0         JNZ      LC1      ; IF E>0 THEN CONTINUE
F0A3 C9             RET               ; ELSE RETURN
```

Figure 13-3. Reassembly with an Entry Point of F086

The next step is to convert this file to a core image file, which has a file suffix of COM. CP/M's dynamic debugger program (DDT) and the SAVE command will do this. DDT is used to read the assembled program into memory starting at address 256, and to convert the assembled program from "hex" format to the binary object code needed. The R (read file from disk) command in DDT will automatically convert FIG13-1.HEX to binary object code, but it will load the program in at address F086H. Since the SAVE command writes consecutive pages of memory to disk beginning with address 256, DDT must also load FIG13-3.HEX beginning at location 256. To do this, you have to calculate an *address offset,* which DDT uses to read the file into memory where you want it to go.

Calculate the offset by using DDT's H command. H, followed by two hexadecimal numbers, will calculate the hexadecimal sum and difference of the two numbers entered. H uses 16-bit arithmetic, and the result, if greater than 0FFFH, will not carry to a fifth digit; rather, it will "roll" to 0000H. To calculate the offset, run DDT:

```
A>DDT
DDT VERS 1.4
-H100 F086 ◄──────── USE H to calculate offset.
F186 107A ◄──────── 107A is the offset.
```

The illustration above shows the H command used for address 100 (256 decimal) and address F086H, the origin point of the subroutine. The second number is the difference; this difference is the offset in the read command. With a difference of 107AH, DDT will begin reading the file into memory starting at address 100H; without the offset value, it would read the file into memory starting at the origin point, F086H. The whole point of this exercise is to read the file, convert it to object code, and use SAVE to write the object code out to disk. The offset factor does not change the addresses used in the assembled program; all it does is relocate the object code at a desired location. In this case, the offset is necessary because SAVE will write from address 100H. The offset may differ for your system, just as the values at addresses 6 and 7 may differ for TPA sizes on other CP/M systems.

Continuing with DDT, the I and R commands are used to read the file into memory:

```
-IFIG13-1.HEX ⎫ ──── Read FIG13-1.HEX into memory
-R107A        ⎬      starting at address 100H.
NEXT  PC      ⎭
011E 0000
```

Now that the file is read into memory, a warm boot operation is executed and the SAVE command is used, allowing for one page of memory:

```
-^C

A>SAVE 1 FIG13-1.COM
A>
```

Using The Assembly Language Subroutine

The file FIG13-3.COM may now be loaded with the following SAVEMEM statement:

SAVEMEM 128,"FIG13-1.COM"

The SADD function can be used to pass the address of the string being converted to lower case. The address of A$, the string to convert, is put in the location reserved for the assembly language subroutine. The CBASIC program in Figure 13-4 will use the assembly language subroutine, and it serves as a good test for your understanding of SAVEMEM procedures.

```
TRUE% = -1
SAVEMEM 128, "FIG13-1.COM"
WHILE TRUE%
        INPUT " STRING TO CONVERT TO LOWER-CASE";LINE STR.DATA$
        IF STR.DATA$ =  "" THEN \REM  NULL STRING - STOP
              TRUE% = 0\
        ELSE \
              POKE 0F086H,  SADD(STR.DATA$) AND 0FFH :\
              POKE 0F087H,  SADD(STR.DATA$)/256 :\
              CALL 0F088H :\
              PRINT "AFTER CONVERSION  ";STR.DATA$
WEND
END
```

Figure 13-4. A CBASIC Program which Interfaces to the Upper-to-Lower Routine Case Conversion

Summary of The Procedure

Here is a brief checklist which you may find handy. Consult it when you want to use an assembly language subroutine with CBASIC programs.

1. Write, test and debug the assembly language subroutine using DDT or another debugging tool.
2. Calculate the end of the TPA by PEEKing locations 6 and 7. (*IMPORTANT: Do not use DDT to display these addresses!* DDT changes addresses 6 and 7, and SAVEMEM will not work with these values. Use PEEK for accurate results.)

3. Calculate the size of the assembly language subroutine in bytes. A short-cut is to ORG the program at address 0 and assemble it. The last address used by the assembler will be the size of the program. Round the size up to the next highest multiple of 128.

4. Assemble the routine at the new origin (highest TPA address minus the size calculated in step 3).

5. Run DDT. Calculate the offset factor using the H command, subtracting the origin used from 100H. Read the .HEX file with the offset. Re-boot CP/M.

6. Use SAVE to write the assembly language routine out to disk. Remember to express the number of pages after SAVE as a multiple of 128.

7. Write the CBASIC interface module. Test the module on a small scale to make sure it works properly and then integrate the module and the assembly language program into your CBASIC applications.

14
CBASIC Statements

THIS CHAPTER DESCRIBES EVERY CBASIC statement in alphabetical order. This summary should be sufficient for an experienced programmer to obtain an understanding of each statement. For more information on any statement refer to the section of this book where the statement is explained in detail.

When a CBASIC statement requires an integer or real expression, an error will occur if a string expression is used. When a statement requires an integer expression, real values will automatically convert to integers; likewise, integer expressions will be converted to real expressions as required. If the statement requires a string expression, an error will occur if the expression is numeric.

TERMS AND ABBREVIATIONS USED IN THIS CHAPTER

The following terms and abbreviations are used in this chapter:

Constant.   Any real number, integer or string with a fixed value.

Delim.   A punctuation mark (either a comma or a semicolon) separating individual items in certain statements and parameter lists.

Expression.   Any single constant, variable or expression.

Integer expression.   Any expression with an integer value.

Numeric expression.   Any expression with an integer or real numeric value.

Parm.   Any item in a statement's parameter list.

Real expression.   Any expression with a real numeric value.

Statement number.   Any valid CBASIC line number.

String expression.   Any expression with a string value.

Variable.   A simple or subscripted variable of any data type, appearing as a single parameter in a statement parameter list.

Braces { }.   Indicate that enclosed parameters may be repeated.

Brackets [ ].   Indicate that enclosed parameters are optional.

ALPHABETIC LIST OF CBASIC STATEMENTS

CALL

The CALL statement is used to link to a machine language subroutine. The CALL statement is normally used in conjunction with the SAVEMEM, PEEK and POKE statements.

Format:

CALL *integer expression*

The expression must evaluate to the address of the subroutine to be executed. When an assembly language return (RET, or object code C9 hexadecimal) instruction is executed, program logic returns to the next sequential CBASIC statement following CALL. CPU registers may be altered by the subroutine without affecting CBASIC.

Examples:

CALL 700H

CALL SUBR%

CHAIN

The CHAIN statement transfers control from the CBASIC program currently being executed to another CBASIC program.

Format:

CHAIN *string expression*

The string expression evaluates to a file name and optional drive specification. The file selected must be of type INT and must exist on the specified drive. When no drive is specified the currently logged-in drive is used. The CHAIN statement causes the selected file to be loaded and the program executed.

A CHAIN statement resets the return stack; any currently open files are closed, and a RESTORE statement executes. Data may be passed from one program to another using the COMMON statement.

Examples:

        CHAIN "MAIN"
        CHAIN "B:SORT"
        CHAIN DRIVE$ + ":" + PRINT.MSG$

CLOSE

The CLOSE statement closes one or more open files.

Format:

        CLOSE *integer expression* { *,integer expression*}

Each expression in the list must represent a file number that is currently open. If the expression does not refer to an active file number, an error will occur. The selected files are closed and the file number is released for future use. Any buffer space being used by the file is returned to the system. If an IF END # statement is currently associated with the file number being closed, the IF END # will no longer be in effect.

Examples:

        CLOSE 1
        CLOSE input.file.id%, temp.file.1%

COMMON

The COMMON statement specifies simple and subscripted variables that are to be common, and therefore retained, when a CHAIN statement is executed.

Format:

        COMMON *variable*{ *,variable*}

Note: If the variable is subscripted, the number of dimensions is placed in parentheses following the variable name, *not* the maximum value of each subscript as in a DIM statement.

If a program has any COMMON statements, they must be the first statements in the program. They may only be preceded by blank lines or REM statements. If a program with COMMON variables executes a CHAIN statement, then the fetched program must have corresponding COMMON statements; that is, each program must have the same number of variables in common, their types must be the same, and if the variable is an array, the number of dimensions must be the same.

Examples:

        COMMON DATE$, NAME$, ACCOUNTS$(1)
        COMMON SIZE%,ACCOUNT.LIMIT(2),COMPANY$

CONSOLE

The CONSOLE statement directs PRINT statement output to the console instead of the printer. CONSOLE is used in conjunction with the LPRINTER statement.

Format:

CONSOLE

The CONSOLE statement redirects output to the console after a prior LPRINTER statement's execution sent PRINT statement output to the printer. If the number of characters printed on the current line of the console exceeds the width, CBASIC issues a carriage return/line feed, thus starting a new line. The default console width is 80 characters. By POKEing a one-byte value to address 272 (or 110 hexadecimal), a new console width may be selected. A zero width is considered infinite and new lines are never automatically started.

The POKE location of 272 assumes that your version of CP/M has a transient program area starting at address 256, or 100 hexadecimal. If your computer (e.g., TRS-80) uses a specially relocated version of CP/M, change the POKE location to the address 16 bytes after the beginning of the TPA.

CREATE

The CREATE statement adds a new file to the directory, then opens the new file. The CREATE statement is similar to the OPEN statement in syntax.

Format:

CREATE *string exression* [RECL *integer expression*] AS *integer expression* [BUFF *integer expression*] [RECS *integer expression*]

The string expression following CREATE is the name of the file to be activated. It must be a valid file name; see Chapter 11 for information on using file names. The integer expression following AS is the file number assigned to this file. The file number is used for later references to the file (see the READ #, PRINT #, IF END #, DELETE and CLOSE statements). The file number must be in the range of 1 to 20 and must not already be in use by another file.

The CREATE statement will retain an IF END # statement executed before the file was created.

The integer expression following RECL, if present, specifies the fixed length of every record in the file. If RECL is omitted, the file will contain variable-length records; variable-length records cannot be accessed randomly. When a record length is specified, the file may be accessed randomly or sequentially. See the PRINT # and READ # statements.

The BUFF and RECS portions of a CREATE statement must always appear together, or not be used at all. The integer expression following BUFF specifies the size of a data buffer for the file, expressed in disk sectors. If BUFF and RECS are omitted, CBASIC assumes a buffer size of one disk sector. Randomly-accessed files cannot have a BUFF value greater than 1. CBASIC presently ignores the integer expression following RECS, but the expression must be present if BUFF is used. For future expansion use the size of a physical sector on the disk. CBASIC currently assumes a sector size of 128 bytes.

Examples:

```
CREATE "LEDGER" AS 3
CREATE FILE.NAME$ RECL S.TEMP% AS FILE.ID% BUFF 10 RECS 128
```

DATA

The DATA statement contains constants which are assigned to variables by READ statements.

Format:

DATA *constant{ ,constant}*

The constants following DATA may be strings, integers or real numbers. A program may include any number of DATA statements, and they may appear anywhere in the program except before a COMMON statement.

A DATA statement must be the only statement on a line. A DATA statement may not be continued using a continuation character. All DATA statements in a program are treated collectively as a list of constants.

DEF

The DEF statement defines either a multiple-line function or a single-line function. The function definition must appear in the program before any reference to the function.

Format for single-line functions:

DEF FN.*name* [(*parm{ ,parm}*)] = *expression*

Format for multiple-line functions:

DEF FN.*name* [(*parm{ ,parm}*)]

The first format is a single-line function. The second format is a multiple-line function, which is used in conjunction with the FEND statement. A multiple-line function consists of the function definition, a body of CBASIC statements, and the FEND statement. A function definition cannot contain a DIM statement, nor can it contain more than one DEF statement.

A function name always begins with the letters FN. The remainder of the name may consist of any number of letters, numbers, and decimal points. No blanks may occur in the name.

The data type of a function is determined by the data type of the function name. Single-line functions evaluate the expression following the equal sign and return the result in the function name.

Multiple-line functions assign values to the function name as if it were a variable; the parameter list is optional here. The value returned by a multiple line function is the latest value assigned to the function name when a RETURN statement executes. The RETURN statement exits the multiple-line function, and passes the latest assignment of the function name to the main program.

Single-line function example:

DEF FN.ADD(A,B)=A+B

Multiple-line function example:

```
DEF FN.TOP.OF.FORM% (HEADING$)
REM Print top-of-form character
PRINT CHR$(OCH);
REM Center the heading on a 132-column page and print it
PRINT TAB(64-(LEN(HEADING$)/2));HEADING$
RETURN
FEND
```

DELETE

The DELETE statement deletes one or more open files.

Format:

DELETE *integer expression* { *,integer expression* }

Each expression in the list must evaluate to a file number that is currently active. If the expression does not refer to an active file number, an error will occur.

The selected files are deleted and the file number is released for future use. All buffer space being used by the file is returned to the system. If an IF END statement is currently associated with the file number being deleted, the IF END will no longer be in effect.

DIM

The DIM statement allocates space for array variables.

Format:

DIM *variable (integer expression{ ,integer expression})*

All array variables must be dimensioned prior to their use. Array variables which are listed in a COMMON statement must still be dimensioned. Numeric arrays are initially set to zero and all elements of string arrays are null strings. If a DIM statement executes more than once for an array, every element of the array is reset to zero or null.

Each subscript has an implied lower bound of zero. The value of each expression is the upper bound for the respective subscript. An array may have any number of subscripts, limited only by your computer's main memory.

Examples:

DIM X(10), Y%(5,5), A$(12,2,2)
DIM W(i%+j%,k%∗10 − e%)

END

The END statement signifies the end of the source program and terminates compilation.

Format:

END

END also performs the functions of a STOP statement. If no END statement is present in a source program, the compiler inserts an END statement when it detects the end of the source file.

FEND

The FEND statement terminates the body of a multiple-line function definition.

Format:

FEND

CBASIC should never execute an FEND statement; all multiple-line functions must end execution with a RETURN statement, otherwise an error will occur. See the DEF statement for more details.

FILE

The FILE statement opens a disk file if the file exists; if the file does not exist, the FILE statement creates it.

Format:

> FILE *string variable* [(*integer expression*)]

The string variable contains the name of the file to open or create. The variable may not be a subscripted variable, a string constant, or an expression. The activated file is assigned the lowest unused file number. File numbers range from 1 through 20; if all twenty available file numbers are already used, an error occurs.

The optional integer expression is the record length of the file. If the record length is omitted, the file will contain variable length records. See the OPEN or CREATE statement for details on the record length and file number.

Examples:

> FILE A$
> FILE FILENAME$(1024)

FOR

The FOR statement begins a FOR/NEXT loop, terminated by a NEXT statement. The FOR statement sets the number of times the loop is to execute, as well as an index value which can ascend or descend in value with each iteration.

Format:

> FOR *variable* = *numeric expression* TO *numeric expression* [STEP expression]

The variable following FOR is the index, which cannot be an array variable. CBASIC evaluates the expression after the equal sign and assigns this value to the index variable.

The expression following TO is the final index value. If the expression after STEP is positive, the loop continues until the the index is greater than the final index value. If the expression after STEP is negative, execution continues until the index is less than the final index value. This final index value is recomputed after each iteration through the loop. The final index value must be an expression of the same type as the index variable.

The expression following STEP is the increment. If STEP is omitted, the increment is set to 1. After each iteration, the increment is calculated and then added to the index. This occurs prior to comparing the index with the termination value.

The index and all expressions used with FOR statements should be integers whenever possible; this will maximize your program's execution speed. Likewise, if an increment value of 1 is desired, the STEP and increment expression should be omitted.

Statements within a FOR/NEXT loop are always executed at least once. See the NEXT statement for additional information.

Examples:

>   FOR I% = 1 TO 10000
>   FOR J = 12.0 TO 123.67 STEP 1.6

GOSUB

The GOSUB statement causes program execution to continue at a specified subroutine statement number. The location of the statement following the GOSUB is stored so that the program can resume after the subroutine completes execution and returns to the main program.

Format:

>   GOSUB *statement number*

The statement number must be a line number elsewhere in the program. The location of the statement following the GOSUB is the return location. It is maintained on a LIFO (last in, first out) stack. The subroutine stack will hold up to 20 return locations at one time.

Examples:

>   GOSUB 200
>   GOSUB 100.001

IF-THEN-ELSE

The IF-THEN-ELSE statement conditionally executes one of two possible statements or groups of statements, depending on the value of an expression or comparison. The conditional expression follows IF. If this expression is non-zero (or true), the statement or statements following THEN will execute; otherwise, the statement or statements following ELSE will execute.

Format:

>   IF *integer expression* THEN *statement* [{: *statement*}]
>   [ELSE *statement* [{: *statement*}]

The statement or statements following THEN will execute if the integer expression has a non-zero value. Comparisons can take the place of the integer expression; if the comparison has a true value, the statements after THEN will execute. If the expression evaluates to zero (or, in the case of a comparison, a false value results), the statement or statements after ELSE will execute. The ELSE is optional; if omitted from the statement, the next sequential CBASIC statement will execute after IF-THEN.

If more than one statement occurs after THEN or ELSE, each statement must be separated by a colon. The following statements may not be used anywhere in the IF-THEN-ELSE statement: DATA, DEF, DIM, IF, and IF END #.

A special form of the IF statement is provided to maintain compatibility with other BASICs. Its format is:

IF *integer expression* THEN *statement number*

This IF statement executes by treating the statement number as a GOTO statement. The ELSE option is not supported with this form of the IF statement.

IF END

IF END # is an error-recovery statement which executes when problems occur during file accessing. These problems include not finding a file, reaching the end of a file, and running out of disk space.

Format:

IF END # *integer expression* THEN *statement number*

The integer expression refers to a file number, between 1 and 20 inclusive. The file does not have to be open in order for this statement to take effect, and the statement number can be any line number elsewhere in the program.

When CBASIC executes the IF END # statement, it sets the error trap and does nothing more. As long as a program executes the IF END # statement somewhere in the program before a file accessing problem happens, a branch will automatically occur to the statement number specified. The IF END statement must be the only statement on a line; it may not follow a colon, nor be part of a list of statements.

When an end of file is detected during a file read, or if an attempt is made to open a file that does not exist, one of two actions will occur. If an IF END # statement has been executed for the file number of the file being accessed, execution of the program continues with the statement number following the THEN in the IF END # statement.

If there is no more disk or directory space available when writing to a file, the IF END # statement will trap this error and branch to the statement specified. Any number of IF END # statements may appear in a program for a given file, but only the most recently executed IF END # is effective. If a DELETE or CLOSE statement is executed, the IF END # associated with the file being deleted or closed is no longer effective.

Examples:

    IF END # 2 THEN 200
    IF END # FILE.ID% THEN 33.3330

INITIALIZE

The INITIALIZE statement resets the operating system's disk directory maps, allowing diskettes to be changed during program execution without restarting the operating system.

Format:

INITIALIZE

If diskettes are changed during a CBASIC program, INITIALIZE must execute after the diskette change is complete. *NEVER* change diskettes while any files are open.

The INITIALIZE statement will re-initialize the usage maps for each disk inserted into every drive on your computer. The drive selected prior to executing the INITIALIZE statement is then reselected.

INPUT

The input statement receives data typed in from the console, assigning the data to one or more variables.

Format:

INPUT ["*message*";] *variable* {, *variable*}

The message is a prompt string, printed on the console device prior to accepting data from the console. The prompt is optional; if omitted, both the prompt and the semicolon must be omitted. When the prompt is not used, a question mark prints on the console to indicate that data should be input from the console. A blank is output following either the question mark or the prompt string. An operator then enters data in response to the prompt or question mark. Prompt strings are directed to the console even when the LPRINTER statement is in effect.

The INPUT statement can receive values for variables of any type, whether simple or subscripted. Each data item entered from the console must be separated by a comma, and the last item entered must be followed by a carriage return. String inputs enclosed in quotation marks will allow commas and leading blanks in the string.

There must be a data item for each variable present in the INPUT statement or CBASIC will request that all data be reentered by printing "IMPROPER INPUT — REENTER". Too many data items or too few will result in this message.

Up to 255 characters may be entered in response to an INPUT statement. Entries longer than this will have the excess portion of the entry truncated to 255 characters. If a control-Z character is the first character entered, the program terminates as though a STOP statement had been executed. Entering control-C will "crash" the program, causing CP/M to re-initialize without closing any disk files which might be open. When entering data, all CP/M line editing functions such as control-U and control-R are in effect.

Examples:

    INPUT "Enter the number of items"; NUM.ITEMS%
    INPUT HEIGHT, WEIGHT, SIZE
    INPUT ""; AMOUNT$

INPUT LINE

The INPUT LINE statement is a special form of the INPUT statement; it reads the entire entry from the console and assigns it to a single string variable.

Format:

    INPUT ["*message*";] LINE *string variable*

The prompt is similar in syntax to the INPUT statement. Only one variable name may appear following the keyword LINE. This variable must be a string variable. After the prompt message or question mark prints, all data entered is assigned to the string variable. The input is terminated with a carriage return which is not included in the string assigned to the variable. Commas and spaces are treated as characters to be included in the string.

A null string may be accepted by responding to an INPUT LINE statement with a carriage return. If more than 255 characters are entered, only the first 255 are accepted. The INPUT LINE statement does not generate an "IMPROPER INPUT" message.

Examples:

    INPUT "Abort? (Y or N)"; LINE ANS$
    INPUT "Type return to continue"; LINE DUMMY$

LET (Assignment Statement)

LET is an optional keyword that precedes an assignment statement. An assignment statement evaluates an expression and assigns the result to a variable.

Format:

    [LET] *variable* = *expression*

The variable may be either simple or subscripted. If the variable is a string, the expression must be a string expression. If the variable is either an integer or real number, the expression must be numeric. The type of a numeric expression will be converted to agree with the type of the variable.

Examples:

LET X = 3
AMOUNT = COST * QTY%
NAME$(I%) = FIRST$(j%) + LAST$(k%)

LPRINTER

The LPRINTER statement directs the output of PRINT statements to the printer. PRINT statement output is normally directed to the console. See the CONSOLE statement.

Format:

LPRINTER [WIDTH *integer expression*]

The optional WIDTH keyword sets the printer width; initially, the width is set at 132 characters. If the current number of characters printed on one line exceeds the width set in the LPRINTER statement, CBASIC issues an automatic carriage return and line feed to the printer. A program can set the width parameter once in an LPRINTER statement, and subsequent LPRINTER statements (omitting the WIDTH parameter) will leave the width unaffected. If the width is set to zero, an infinite width is assumed.

Examples:

LPRINTER
LPRINTER WIDTH PRINTER.WIDTH%
LPRINTER WIDTH 0

NEXT

The NEXT statement terminates a FOR/NEXT loop; see the discussion on the FOR statement.

Format:

NEXT [*variable* { ,*variable* }]

The NEXT statement marks the end of its companion FOR statement. If the optional list of index variables is present, the FOR and NEXT statement indexes must match for each loop being terminated. If a NEXT statement index does not match with a FOR statement, an error occurs.

More than one FOR statement loop may be terminated by a single NEXT statement by using more than one index variable. A single NEXT statement with multiple indexes has the same effect as multiple NEXT statements, each with one index. When NEXT executes, the index variable increments by 1 or by the increment specified after STEP (if STEP is used), and the program branches back to its matching FOR statement expression of the corresponding FOR statement. Then the index is tested to see if loop exit criteria have been met. See the FOR statement.

After exiting the loop, the statement directly following NEXT is executed.

Examples:

    NEXT
    NEXT A%
    NEXT INDEX%, LOOP.VARIABLE%, FOR.NEXT.ITERATION%

ON GOTO

The ON GOTO statement branches program execution to one of several statement numbers, depending on the value of an expression.

Format:

    ON *integer expression* GOTO *statement number* { ,*statement number* }

The value of the expression selects which line number to branch to from those listed in the statement. An error occurs if the expression is less than or equal to zero, or if the expression is larger than the number of statement numbers present.

Examples:

    ON I% GOTO 100, 200, 300
    ON CODE% − 3 GOTO 33.1, 33.2, 33.3

ON GOSUB

The ON GOSUB statement is similar to the ON GOTO statement described above. A GOSUB is executed to the selected statement number. When a RETURN is executed for the GOSUB, control is transferred to the statement that directly follows ON GOSUB.

Format:

    ON *integer expression* GOSUB *statement number* { ,*statement number* }

OPEN

The OPEN statement is used to activate a disk file for accessing. The OPEN statement is similar to the CREATE statement.

Format:

> OPEN *string expression* [RECL *integer expression*] AS *integer expression*
> [BUFF *integer expression* RECS *integer expression*]

The string expression following OPEN is the name of the file to activate; it must be a valid file name. The integer expression following AS is the file number assigned to this file. The file number is used for subsequent references to the file. See the READ #, PRINT #, IF END #, DELETE and CLOSE statements. The file number must be in the range of 1 to 20 and must not be used currently by another file.

The OPEN statement has no effect on any IF END # statements currently in effect for the newly opened file number. If the file to be opened does not exist, the statement number associated with the IF END # currently in effect for this file will be executed. If no IF END # statement is in effect for the file number, an error will occur.

The integer expression following RECL, if present, specifies the record length. If RECL is omitted, the file will contain variable-length records. When a record length is specified, the file has fixed-length records which may be accessed, randomly or sequentially. See the PRINT # and READ # statements.

The BUFF and RECS portions of an OPEN statement must always appear together, or not be used at all. The integer expression following BUFF specifies the number of disk sectors to be maintained in memory. If BUFF and RECS are omitted, CBASIC assumes a buffer size of 1 sector (BUFF 1). Files opened for random access cannot have a BUFF value greater than 1. The expression following RECS is currently ignored, but it must be present if BUFF is used. For future expansion use the size of a physical sector on the disk. The system currently assumes a sector size of 128 bytes.

Examples:

> OPEN "LEDGER" AS 3
> OPEN FILE.NAME$ RECL S.TEMP% AS F.ID% BUFF 10 RECS 128

OUT

The OUT statement outputs an 8-bit integer value to an input/output port using standard 8080A/Z80A microprocessor I/O port addressing.

Format:

> OUT *integer expression,integer expression*

The low-order byte of the second expression is sent to the output port addressed by the low-order byte of the first expression.

Examples:
> OUT 3, 80H
> OUT TAPE.DATA%, NEXT.CHAR%

POKE

The POKE statement places one byte of data in a selected memory location.

Format:
> POKE *integer expression,integer expression*

The low-order byte of the second expression is stored at the memory location determined by the first expression.

Examples:
> POKE 100H, 255
> POKE MSG.ID%, END.MARK%

PRINT

The PRINT statement outputs data to the console or printer (see the LPRINTER and CONSOLE statements). Any combination of strings or numeric expressions may be printed.

Format:
> PRINT *expression* {*delim expression*} [*delim*]

If CBASIC prints a real numeric variable less than 0.1 or more than 15 digits long, the value prints in scientific notation with one digit to the left of the decimal point. Strings are output with no modifications. If the length of a numeric value would result in the line width being exceeded, the number is printed on the next line. Strings are output until the line width is reached and then the remainder of the string, if any, is output on the next line.

The delimiter between expressions may be either a comma (,) or a semicolon (;). A comma causes tabulation to the next column that is a multiple of 20: that is to column 20, 40, 60, etc. If this tabbing results in the line width being exceeded, a carriage return and line feed are output. A semicolon causes one blank character to be output before a numeric value, and no spacing to occur after a string.

The delimiter at the end of the PRINT statement is optional. If it is present it must be either a comma or semicolon. The comma and semicolon have the same effect described above. No carriage return is output if the PRINT statement ends in a delimiter. The delimiter at the end of a PRINT statement has the effect of allowing the next PRINT statement to continue where the previous one left off. If no delimiter is used, a carriage return and line feed are output after all the expressions have been printed.

A PRINT statement with no parameter list will cause a carriage return and line feed to be output.

Examples:

```
PRINT VALUE, AMOUNT
PRINT "The amount owed is"; COST
PRINT A$; B$, C$;
PRINT
```

PRINT

The PRINT # statement outputs data to disk files. The PRINT and PRINT # statements function similarly, as described above, except all PRINT # output is directed to a disk file.

Format:

PRINT # *integer expression* [,*integer expression*]; *expression*{ ,*expression*}

The PRINT # statement has two parts: the file and record selector, terminated with the semicolon, and the list of expressions to write to the disk file. These expressions are separated by commas, but commas may not appear at the end of the PRINT # statement parameter list.

The file and record selector identifies which file and record to access. The first expression is the file number, identifying the file to which data will be output. This must be an active file number in the range of 1 to 20. The second expression is optional. If present it is the record number to which data is printed. Thus the second expression specifies a relative file record access. Relative files must be opened with the RECL option. See the OPEN and CREATE statements for further reference.

Numeric expressions are output to the file with the same format used when printing to the console. CBASIC encloses strings in quotation marks before being output. Strings being output to a disk file should not contain quotation mark characters within the string. Every data item in the PRINT # parameter list is separated by a comma when output to the file. The last item in the list is followed by a carriage return and a line feed instead of a comma. If fixed length records are selected, blanks pad the unused part of the record and the line feed is the last character in the record.

Examples:

PRINT # 1; A,B,C

PRINT # DATA%, REC.NO%; NAME$,STREET$,CITY$,STATE$,ZIP$

PRINT USING

The PRINT USING statement provides formatted output to the console or the printer. The required format is described using a format expression.

Format:

PRINT USING *string expression;expression* {*;expression*}

The string expression is a format string which consists of data templates and literal characters. The literal characters are printed as they appear in the format string. The data template describes the format to use when outputting a value from the expression list.

The following characters make up data templates:

#	Numeric digit. Mark one digit in output of a number.
^	Exponent. Indicate number in exponential format.
.	Decimal point. Mark location of decimal point.
—	Mark position for sign of number. May be trailing or leading.
,	Comma insertion. Require comma insertion every three digits before decimal point.
$$	Leading dollar sign. Put floating dollar sign on number.
**	Asterisk fill. Fill field with leading asterisks.
!	String character. Output first character of string variable.
/	String field. Mark beginning and end of string field.
\	Escape character. Treat the next character in the format expression as a literal character.

Examples:

PRINT USING " # # # # # # # / / "; X, Y, A$

PRINT USING "The amount due is $$#,###.## "; TOTAL.DUE

PRINT USING

The PRINT USING # statement outputs formatted data to disk files. See the PRINT # and PRINT USING statements for details on formatted printing and printing to a disk file.

Example:

PRINT USING "# # # # /....../ # #"; #1,RECORD.NUMBER%;
ITEM%,NAME$,CODE%

RANDOMIZE

The RANDOMIZE statement is used to seed the random number generator.

Format:

RANDOMIZE

An operator's input response time following execution of an INPUT statement is used to seed the random number generator. Thus an INPUT statement should be executed prior to executing a RANDOMIZE statement.

READ

The READ statement assigns values from DATA statements to variables. The values in DATA statements are used sequentially as they appear in the program. See the DATA and RESTORE statements.

Format:

READ *variable{ ,variable}*

Examples:

READ COST1,COST2,COST3
READ TABLE(I%)

READ

The READ # statement reads data from disk files. It functions similarly to the READ statement described above, except all data is read from a disk file.

Format:

READ # *integer expression* [,*integer expression*]; *variable* { ,*variable}*

The READ # statement consists of two parts: the file and record selector portion, terminated with the semicolon, and the variable list. The file and record selector portion of the READ # statement functions as described for the PRINT # statement. The first expression selects which file number to read, and the optional second expression selects the record number for a random access. If the second expression is not used, the next record in the file is read.

The record selector can only be used if the file being accessed has fixed-length records and was opened with the RECL parameter. See the CREATE, FILE and OPEN statements for more information.

When an attempt is made to read past the end of file, execution continues with the statement number in the last IF END # executed for this file number. If no IF END # has been executed, an error occurs.

For each variable in the list the next field in the record is read and assigned to the variable. A field is always delimited by a comma or carriage return. If an attempt is made to read past a carriage return for a file which was activated with the RECL option, an error occurs.

Examples:

    READ # 1; NEXT.DATA.ITEM$
    READ # FILE.NUMBER%,RECORD.NUMBER%; NAME$(1)

READ # LINE

The READ # LINE statement reads one record from the selected file and assigns it to a string variable. The READ # LINE statement is similar to the READ # statement.

Format:

    READ # *integer expression* [,*integer expression*]; *string variable*

The file and record selector portion of the READ # LINE statement is identical to the READ # statement. The first expression selects the file and the optional second expression selects a relative file. The string variable will be set equal to the record read from the file. If the length of the record is greater than 255 bytes, the record is truncated to 255 characters and a warning is printed on the console.

REM

All characters to the right of a REM statement are ignored and treated as a remark. The REM statement is used to document programs.

Format:

    REM *any characters*

The REM statement may be continued to the next line with a backslash. REM statements are ignored by the compiler; the size of the intermediate language file produced by the compiler is not affected by REM statements. A REM statement that is part of a group of statements on the same line must be the last statement in the group.

Examples:

REM   This remark is on one line

REM \

This \

remark can be longer \

than one line if a backslash is used.

REMARK

The REMARK statement is identical to the REM statement.

RESTORE

The RESTORE statement resets the pointer in the DATA statement area to the beginning of the data list. The next READ statement will then access the first item in the first DATA statement.

Format:

RESTORE

See the DATA statement and READ statement.

RETURN

The RETURN statement causes program execution to continue with the statement following the most recently executed GOSUB statement or user-defined function reference.

Format:

RETURN

Each GOSUB statement saves the location of the statement following the GOSUB so that the program can return from the GOSUB. Likewise, when a user-defined function is referenced, the location to which the calculated value must be returned is saved. A return causes execution to continue at the most recently saved location. See the GOSUB, ON GOSUB, and DEF statements.

SAVEMEM

The SAVEMEM statement reserves space for a file. The file is loaded when the

SAVEMEM statement is executed. The file is normally a machine language subroutine.

Format:

SAVEMEM *integer constant,string expression*

The integer constant specifies the number of bytes of memory to reserve for the file being loaded. The space is reserved at the top of the transient program area. The beginning address of the reserved area is calculated by taking the integer constant and subtracting it from the largest available address.

The string expression specifies the file to read. Records are read from the file until either an end of file is encountered or the next record to be read exceeds the available memory. If the string expression is null or the integer constant is less than 128, space is reserved but no file is loaded.

Only one SAVEMEM statement may appear in a program. If the first program executed has a SAVEMEM statement, then any chained program must have a SAVEMEM statement with the same integer constant. A different file may be loaded by each chained program.

Examples:

SAVEMEM 1028, "IOPACK.COM"
SAVEMEM 128, ""

STOP

The STOP statement causes program execution to stop. Control is returned to CP/M.

Format:

STOP

Any open files are closed.

WEND

The WEND statement terminates a WHILE statement loop. See the WHILE statement below.

Format:

WEND

WHILE

The WHILE statement controls looping between the WHILE statement and a corresponding WEND statement.

Format:

> WHILE *integer expression*

Looping continues until the integer expression is a value other than -1; that is, until the expression is false. The loop may contain any number of statements, including other WHILE statements. If the expression is false initially, no statements in the loop will be executed.

Examples:

> WHILE AMOUNT $<=$ MAX
> WHILE -1 REM LOOP FOREVER

15
CBASIC Functions

THIS CHAPTER WILL summarize every CBASIC function as alphabetized by function keyword. The summary provides an overview of the function and should be sufficient information for experienced programmers. This chapter should be used by beginners to obtain a complete and accurate definition of every function encountered in earlier chapters.

A function that requires an integer or real expression will generate an error if the expression evaluates to a string. When an integer expression is required, real values are converted to integer. Likewise, integer expressions are converted to real expressions, as required. If an argument requires a string expression, an error will occur if the expression is numeric.

ALPHABETIC LIST OF CBASIC FUNCTIONS

ABS

The ABS function returns the absolute value of the argument.

Format:

ABS(numeric expression)

The expression must be numeric.

Examples:

```
X = ABS(Y)
DIFF = ABS(COST − PROFIT)
```

ASC

The ASC function returns an integer value equal to the ASCII code for the first character of the argument.

Format:

```
ASC(string expression)
```

ASC only returns the value of the first character in the expression. If the expression evaluates to a null string an error will occur.

Examples:

```
I% = ASC(STRING$)
FIRST% = ASC(FIRST.NAME$)
```

ATN

The ATN function returns the arctangent of the argument.

Format:

```
ATN(numeric expression)
```

The argument must be expressed in radians. Other inverse trigonometric functions may be computed by using the arctangent. The value returned is a real number.

Examples:

```
ANGLE = ATN(X)
ASIN = ATN(X/SQR(1.0 − X * X))
```

CHR$

The CHR$ function converts the argument to a single character string.

Format:

CHR$(numeric expression)

The argument is assumed to be an ASCII code. The function returns the ASCII character represented by the argument. If the argument is greater than 255, the high-order byte is ignored.

Examples:

BELL$ = CHR$(7)
PRINT CHR$ (TOP.OF.FORM%);

COMMAND$

The COMMAND$ function returns the command line which was used to execute the program.

Format:

COMMAND$

The string returned does not include the "CRUN2" directive, the name of the program being executed, or the directive "TRACE" if the trace option is being used. For instance, if a program is executed with the following command line:

CRUN2 LEDGER DIABLO 80

COMMAND would return a string containing "DIABLO 80."

The COMMAND$ function allows options to be passed to a CBASIC program when it is executed. The COMMAND$ function may be used anywhere, and as often as needed, in the originally executed program, and in any program subsequently loaded by a CHAIN statement.

CONCHAR%

The CONCHAR% predefined function waits for and accepts one character from the console.

Format:

CONCHAR%

The CONCHAR% function returns an integer equal to the binary representation of the character read from the console. The CONCHAR% function echoes the character read back to the console. If no character has been entered at the console, CONCHAR% returns a 0. See the CONSTAT% function.

Examples:

    ANS% = CONCHAR%
    IF CONCHAR% = ESC% THEN DONE% = TRUE%

CONSTAT%

The CONSTAT% function returns a −1 (true) if a character has been entered at the console, and a 0 (false) if no character is pending.

Format:

    CONSTAT%

The CONSTAT% function returns an integer equal to the status of the console. If the console has a character ready, true (−1) is returned, otherwise false (0) is returned.

Examples:

    IF CONSTAT% THEN ANS% = CONCHAR%
    X% = CONSTAT%

COS

The COS function returns the cosine of the argument.

Format:

    COS(numeric expression)

The argument must be expressed in radians. The value returned is a real number.

Example:

    X = COS(ANGLE)

EXP

The EXP function returns the value of the constant *e* raised to the power represented by the argument.

Format:

    EXP(numeric expression)

The value returned is a real number.

Examples:

POWER = EXP(X*X − Y*Y)

E = EXP(1)

FLOAT

The FLOAT function converts the argument to a real number.

Format:

FLOAT(numeric expression)

If the argument is already a real number, FLOAT converts the argument to an integer and then back to a real number.

Examples:

X = SIN(FLOAT(I%))

FRE

The FRE function returns the number of bytes not being used in the dynamic or free storage area.

Format:

FRE

The value returned by FRE is a real number equal to the total amount of space that is not being used. The space in the free storage area may not be one contiguous area of memory.

Example:

SPACE.REMAINING = FRE

INP

The INP function returns a byte from a selected input/output port.

Format:

INP(integer expression)

The INP function returns an integer which is the value read from the port addressed by the argument.

Examples:

```
DEV.1% = INP(23)
TAPE.STATUS% = INP(TAPE.SP%)
```

INT

The INT function truncates the fractional part of an argument, returning only the integer portion. If the argument is a real number, it is first converted to an integer, and then is converted back to a real number.

Format:

```
INT(numeric expression)
```

The value returned by INT is a real number. See the INT% function also.

Examples:

```
DOLLARS = INT(TOTAL.DUE)
CENTS = TOTAL − INT(TOTAL.DUE)
```

INT%

The INT% function converts the argument to an integer.

Format:

```
INT%(numeric expression)
```

The difference between INT and INT% is that the result of INT is an integer value stored in memory as a real number, while the result of INT% is an integer.

Examples:

```
K% = INT%(DATA.IN)
LENGTH = ARRAY.VAR(INT%(X))
```

LEFT$

The LEFT$ function returns the leftmost characters of the argument.

Format:

> LEFT$(string expression , numeric expression)

The numeric expression specifies the number of characters to be returned. If the number of characters to be returned is greater than the length of the string expression, the entire first argument is returned. If the numeric expression is zero, a null string is returned; if it is negative, an error will occur.

Examples:

> RESPONSE$ = LEFT$(ANS$,1)
> PRINT LEFT$(NAME$,MAX.NAME.LENGTH%)

LEN

The LEN function returns the number of characters in a string expression.

Format:

> LEN(string expression)

The LEN function will return zero for a null string.

Examples:

> LENGTH.NAME% = LEN(NAME$)
> IF LEN(TEMP$) >= MAX.L% THEN GOTO 100.00

LOG

The LOG function returns the natural logarithm of the argument.

Format:

> LOG(numeric expression)

The LOG function can be used to calculate logarithms to other bases. An error occurs if the argument is negative or zero.

Examples:

> BASE.TEN.L = LOG(X)/LOG(10)
> Z = LOG(W)

MATCH

The MATCH function returns the first occurrence of a pattern string in a source string, starting the search at a specific character position in the source string.

Format:

> MATCH(string expression, string expression, numeric expression)

The first argument is the pattern; the second argument is the source string. The third argument specifies the position in the source string, or second argument, where the search is to start. The search progresses from the starting position to the end of the source string, attempting to match the pattern. If a match occurs, the position of the first matching character in the source is returned. If no match occurs, a zero is returned.

The following pattern matching override characters are provided:

#	A pound sign will match any numeric digit (0-9).
!	An exclamation mark will match any upper- or lower-case letter (A-Z and a-z).
?	A question mark will match any character.
\	A backslash indicates that the character following the backslash does not have special meaning. Thus a backslash before a #, !, ?, or another backslash will override the definition above and result in the character being ignored as a special pattern character.

If either string expression is null, a zero is returned. If the starting position for the match is greater than the length of the source string, a zero is returned. If the numeric expression is zero or negative, an error occurs.

Examples:

> MATCH("CDE","ABCDEFGHI",1) returns 3
> MATCH("CDE","ABCDEFGHI",3) returns 3
> MATCH("CDE","ABCDEFGHI",4) returns 0
> MATCH("D?F","ABCDEFGHI",1) returns 4
> MATCH("\ #1\\\?","1#1\?2#",1) returns 2

MID$

The MID$ function returns a string that is a portion of a string argument. The MID$ function can replace either the RIGHT$ function or the LEFT$ function, but in addition MID$ can return a string taken from the middle of another string.

Format:

> MID$(string expression, numeric expression, numeric expression)

A portion of the first argument will be returned, based on the values of the second and third arguments. The second argument identifies the first character of the string to return. The third argument specifies the length of the returned string. If the third argument would extend the returned string beyond the length of the string argument, all characters from the starting position to the actual end of string are returned. If the starting position is greater than the length of the string argument, a null string is returned. If the third argument is zero, a null string is returned.

If either of the numeric arguments is negative or the second argument is zero, an error will occur.

Examples:

```
MIDDLE$ = MID$(NAME$,START.MN%,LENGTH.MN%)
DAY$ = MID$("MONTUEWEDTHUFRISATSUN",DAY%*3-2,3)
```

PEEK

The PEEK function returns the contents of a selected memory location.

Format:

```
PEEK(numeric expression)
```

The argument represents a memory location. The PEEK function returns an integer value equal to the contents of that memory location. The memory location must be within the address space of the computer being used.

For memory locations greater than 32767 the argument must be negative, in which case the argument should be expressed in hexadecimal notation for clarity.

Examples:

```
BDOS% = PEEK(6) + PEEK(7)*256
ENTRY% = PEEK(0E00H)
PARM1% = PEEK(LOC.P1%)
```

POS

The POS function returns the column position where the next character output will be printed.

Format:

```
POS
```

The value returned by the POS function is an integer. If an LPRINTER statement is in effect, POS will return the next position to be printed on the printer, otherwise the value POS returns will be the cursor position of the console.

POS actually returns the number of characters that have been printed since the last carriage return and linefeed, plus one. If the cursor has been postioned by special characters, or any nonprinting characters have been output, the POS function will not return the actual cursor position.

Examples:

```
PRINT TAB(POS+3); "#"
LOC.CURSOR% = POS
```

RENAME

The RENAME function changes the name of a disk file.

Format:

```
RENAME(string expression1, string expression 2)
```

String expression 1 is the new name for the file; string expression 2 is the name of the file to be changed. The RENAME function returns an integer value of zero if the rename fails. −1 is returned if the rename is successful.

The file being renamed must not be open. If an open file is renamed, an error will occur when the file is closed.

Examples:

```
IF RENAME("MASTER.CUR","MASTER.TMP") = 0 THEN GOTO 500
X% = RENAME(NEW.NAME$,OLD.NAME$)
```

RIGHT$

The RIGHT$ function returns the rightmost characters of the argument.

Format:

```
RIGHT$(string expression, numeric expression)
```

The numeric expression specifies the number of characters to extract from the string expression. If the number of characters to be returned is greater than the length of the string expression, the entire first argument will be returned. If the numeric expression is zero, a null string will be returned and if it is negative an error will occur.

Examples:

    CHECK.DIGIT$ = RIGHT$(ACCOUNT.NO$,1)
    LAST.NAME$ = RIGHT$(NAME$,LEN(NAME$)-LEN(FIRST.NAME$))

RND

The RND function returns a random real number between 0 and 1.

Format:

    RND

The RND function will generate the next random number based on the current seed. The value returned is a real number. See the RANDOMIZE statement for information on seeding the random number generator.

Example:

    PRINT RND

SADD

The SADD function returns the address in memory where a string variable is stored. The first byte of the string holds the string character length. String characters follow the length byte.

Format:

    SADD(string variable)

The argument must be a string variable name. An expression is not permitted. The value returned by SADD is an integer. A zero may be returned for a null string, however some null strings have addresses other than zero, even though their length is zero.

If the location of the string is at an address greater than 32767, the integer is returned with a negative value. However, the address is valid and may be passed to an assembly language routine using the PEEK function and the POKE statement.

Examples:

    LOC.PARM% = SADD(NAME$)
    PTR% = SADD(A$)

SGN

The SGN function returns either a −1, 0, or 1 depending on whether the argument is negative, zero, or positive.

Format:

SGN(numeric expression)

The value returned is an integer.

Examples:

IF SGN(TOTAL) = −1 THEN GOSUB 200.20
ON SGN(X) + 2 GOTO 10, 20, 30

SIN

The SIN function returns the sine of the argument.

Format:

SIN(numeric expression)

The argument must be expressed in radians. The value returned is a real number.

Example:

X = SIN(ANGLE)

SIZE

The SIZE function returns the amount of space reserved for a file or a group of files.

Format:

SIZE(string expression)

The string expression may be an ambiguous file name, or the name of one file in the directory. If an ambiguous file name is specified, the space used by all files selected by the ambiguous name is returned.

If no files in the directory match the expression, zero is returned. The SIZE function returns an integer, equal to the number blocks used. One block is eight 128-byte sectors (i.e., 1024 bytes).

Examples:

AMOUNT% = SIZE(WORKFILE)
I% = SIZE("*.BAK")
FREE.SPACE% = DISK.CAPACITY% − SIZE("*.*")

SQR

The SQR function returns the square root of the argument.

Format:

SQR(real expression)

The SQR function returns a real number. If the argument is negative, a warning is displayed and the absolute value of the argument is used to calculate the square root.

Examples:

HYP = SQR(X*X + Y*Y)
PRINT SQR(X)

STR$

The STR$ function returns a character string equivalent to the argument.

Format:

STR$(numeric expression)

The numeric expression is converted to a character string. This string is identical to the characters that would be printed if the numeric expression were displayed.

Examples:

A$ = STR$(X)
PRINT STR$(ZIP)

TAB

The TAB function positions the cursor to the column specified by the argument.

Format:

TAB(integer expression)

The TAB function may only be used in PRINT statements. The cursor or printer, depending on whether LPRINTER is in effect, is moved right to the selected column. If the expression is less than the current position, a new line is started, and then the TAB occurs. The tab will not move backwards.

If the argument exceeds the line width of the current output device, an error occurs. A semicolon should be used following a tab. A comma causes additional spacing.

Examples:

```
PRINT TAB(START.COL%);NAME$
PRINT X;TAB(30);Y
```

UCASE$

The UCASE$ function converts all lower-case letters in a string to upper-case.

Format:

```
UCASE$(string expression)
```

The value returned by UCASE$ is a string. Each lower-case alphabetic character in the argument is converted to an upper-case character.

Other characters in the argument are not modified.

Examples:

```
U.CITY$ = UCASE$(CITY$)
X$ = UCASE$(X$)
```

VAL

The VAL function converts a string into a real number.

Format:

```
VAL(string expression)
```

The real number returned by VAL equals the number represented by the string expression. This conversion is equivalent to numeric keyboard input to an INPUT statement.

Examples:

```
X = VAL(A$)
PI = VAL("3.1416")
```

VARPTR

The VARPTR function returns the *permanent* storage location assigned to a variable.

Format:

> VARPTR(variable)

The variable may be either a numeric or string variable. If the variable is numeric, VARPTR passes the address of the numeric variable. If the variable is a string the address returned contains a pointer to the string currently assigned to the variable.

Examples:

```
POKE PARMLOC%, LOW (VARPTR(X))
POKE PARMLOC%+1,HIGH (VARPTR(X))
```

16
Using CBASIC

THIS CHAPTER DESCRIBES the use of the CBASIC compiler, CBAS2, and the cross reference lister, XREF. The CBASIC compiler provides command line toggles and special compiler directives to modify the listings and support chaining. The cross reference lister will produce an alphabetical listing of all variables used in a program, along with each line number that references the variable.

COMMAND LINE OPTIONS

The CBASIC Compiler, CBAS2, is executed by typing CBAS2 and the name of the source program to compile. The source program name must have a type of "BAS." For example, to compile the program TEST.BAS type:

            CBAS2 TEST

The CBASIC compiler will read the file TEST.BAS from the currently active CP/M drive and produce an intermediate file TEST.INT on the same drive. In addition, a listing of the source file will be printed on the console. Following the listing will be some statistical data relating to the program. The following CBASIC program:

            REM TEST PROGRAM
            INPUT X
            100 Y = 2.0 * X
            PRINT X,Y

is compiled by typing the command:

            CBAS2 TEST

The listing produced on the console is shown in Figure 16-1. Note that each line in the program has been assigned a line number by CBASIC. This line number has no relation to statement labels or numbers assigned by the programmer. For instance, on the third line the programmer assigned the label 100 to that statement. The 100 in line 3 is a statement number. In Figure 16-1 the line numbers are followed by a colon, except in the case of line 3. The asterisk indicates that the statement number (100) used in line 3 is never referenced in the program. This allows you to eliminate unused statement numbers, increasing the readability of CBASIC programs.

If the source file is on a different drive than the currently active CP/M drive, the source file name must have a drive reference. For instance, if TEST.BAS were on drive B, the following command would compile TEST.BAS:

CBAS2 B:TEST

In this case the intermediate file TEST.INT will be placed on drive B.

The intermediate file may be placed on a different drive from the drive the source file is on by placing a drive assignment after the source file name. For example:

CBAS2 TEST B:

will place the intermediate file TEST.INT on drive B. The source file resides on CP/M's currently active drive. The disk reference must follow the source file name and be separated from it with at least one blank. It must precede any toggles that may be used.

```
A>CBAS2 TEST
CBASIC COMPILER VER 2.07
    1: REM TEST PROGRAM
    2:        X = 4.5
    3* 100    Y = 2.0 * X
    4:        PRINT X,Y
    5: END
NO ERRORS DETECTED
CONSTANT AREA:      24
CODE SIZE:          25
DATA STMT AREA:      0
VARIABLE AREA:      16
```

Figure 16-1. Compiler Output of TEST.BAS Without Toggles

COMMAND LINE TOGGLES

You can control the operation of CBAS2 by placing *toggles* on the command line. The toggles are either upper- or lower-case characters. A dollar sign precedes the first toggle to mark the beginning of the command line toggles. The list of toggles must be the last part of the command line. For example, the following command line uses toggles:

CBAS2 TEST $BE

B, C, D, E, F, and G are valid toggles. Other characters are ignored.

The B Toggle

The B toggle suppresses the listing of the source file to the console. However, the compiler statistics always list on the console. Figure 16-2 shows the output to the console when TEST.BAS (from Figure 16-1) is compiled with the following command:

CBAS2 TEST $B

When the B toggle is used, errors found in the source program will print on the console, but the source line associated with the error will not be listed. Figure 16-3 shows the results of compiling TEST.BAS after modifying it to cause an error message.

The C Toggle

The C toggle suppresses the creation of an intermediate file. This will result in somewhat faster compilations when checking for errors in a program. You would use this toggle to check for compiler errors in a program.

```
A>CBAS2 TEST $B
CBASIC COMPILER VER 2.07
NO ERRORS DETECTED
CONSTANT AREA:      24
CODE SIZE:          25
DATA STMT AREA:      0
VARIABLE AREA:      16
```

Figure 16-2. Compilation of TEST.BAS With $B Toggle

The D Toggle

The D toggle will suppress the automatic translation of lower-case letters, used in variable names, to upper-case. Thus, when the D toggle is used the variable names "PAY" and "pay" are treated as different variables. When the D toggle is used, all reserved words must be in upper-case. The word "print" would not be treated as a reserved word in a program compiled with the D toggle.

The E Toggle

The E toggle is used to help debug programs. When the E toggle is used, additional information is included in the intermediate file so that execution errors cause the source line number that was being executed to be listed with the error message. These line numbers are the numbers the compiler assigns to each source line. They have no relationship to numbers the programmer may use as labels to statements.

The E toggle is also necessary if you want to use the TRACE option when running a CBASIC program.

The F Toggle

The F toggle produces a listing of the program on the printer in addition to the listing on the console. The only difference between the listing on the printer and that on the console is that each page listed to the printer will have a title line, and at the end of the page a form feed character (ASCII OCH) is generated to position the paper to the top of the next sheet. The command line:

> CBAS2 TEST $F

will produce the listing shown in Figure 16-3.

```
          CBASIC V2.07 COMPILATION OF TEST

          1: REM TEST PROGRAM
          2:        X = 4.5
          3* 100    Y = 2.0 * X
          4:        PRINT S,Y
          5: END
          NO ERRORS DETECTED
          CONSTANT AREA:     24
          CODE SIZE:         25
          DATA STMT AREA:     0
          VARIABLE AREA:     16
```

Figure 16-3. Compiler Output Listing of TEST.BAS
Using $G Toggle

The information provided after COMPILATION OF in each heading line is taken from the command line following the CBAS2. *All* characters from the beginning of the program name to either the end of the command line or up to the dollar sign will print in the title line. For instance:

CBAS2 TEST ON 24 MAY 1981 $F

would produce the title line shown in Figure 16-4.

The G Toggle

The G toggle produces a listing to a disk file. The listing file is identical to that listed on the console (unless the B toggle is also used).

COMPILER DIRECTIVES

Compiler directives are special CBASIC statements which direct the compiler itself to take some specific action. The directives do not affect the execution of the program. All compiler directives start with a percent sign followed by the name of the directive. There may be no spaces between the percent sign and the directive name. In addition, the directive must start in the first column of a source line. No line number may be used with a compiler directive.

The first four directives, %LIST, %NOLIST, %PAGE, and %EJECT, control the format of the listing produced by the compiler. Normally the source program is listed on the console as it is compiled. If a compiler toggle is selected to create a listing on the printer, or onto a disk file, the listing control directives can be used to format the listing.

```
CBASIC V2.07 COMPILATION OF TEST ON 24 MAY 1981

    1:  REM TEST PROGRAM
    2:          X = 4.5
    3* 100      Y = 2.0 * X
    4:          PRINT X,Y
    5:  END
NO ERRORS DETECTED
CONSTANT AREA:      24
CODE SIZE:          25
DATA STMT AREA:      0
VARIABLE AREA:      16
```

Figure 16-4. $G Toggle Compilation With a Title Line

%LIST and %NOLIST

The %LIST and %NOLIST directives turn the listing on and off. This allows selected portions of a program not to be listed. For example:

```
REM ROUTINE TO PRINT RECORD
%NOLIST
PRINT #FILE.NO% ;NAME$,ACCOUNT.NO%,AMOUNT.DUE
%LIST
```

will not list the third line above. The listing will look like this:

```
1:   REM ROUTINE TO PRINT RECORD
2:   %NOLIST
4:   %LIST
```

The %LIST and %NOLIST directives affect output to the console as well as to the printer or a disk file.

%EJECT and %PAGE

The %EJECT directive positions the printer to the top of the next sheet of paper. To operate properly, the printer must accept form feed (ASCII OCH) characters. The %EJECT directive has no effect on listings to disk files or to the console.

The %PAGE directive sets the number of lines to be printed on each page when printing to the printer. CBASIC defaults to 64 lines per printed page. The %PAGE directive requires an integer constant to be provided following the directive. For example:

```
%PAGE(40)
```

will set the page length to 40. After 40 lines have been printed a form feed character is sent to the printer. The %PAGE directive has no effect on listings printed on the console, or directed to a disk file.

Two compiler directives — %INCLUDE and %CHAIN — control the compilation process itself.

%INCLUDE DIRECTIVE

The %INCLUDE directive allows other CBASIC programs to be included in the current program being compiled. The statements in the "included" file are treated as if they appeared in the program being compiled. For example:

```
%INCLUDE DISKDEF
```

will include the file DISKDEF.BAS into a CBASIC program. The file to be included may be located on any drive. For example:

```
%INCLUDE B:DISKDEF
```

will include the file DISKDEF.BAS from drive B. Any file included must be of type BAS.

The listing produced by CBASIC will replace the colon following the line number with an equal sign (=) if the statement has been included from another file. For example, the subroutine:

```
REM PRINT A RECORD
%INCLUDE RECDEF
RETURN
```

would be listed:

```
1:   REM PRINT A RECORD
2:   %INCLUDE RECDEF
3=   PRINT #2; ACCOUNT.NO%,NAME$,AMOUNT
4:   RETURN
```

In this example the file RECDEF.BAS contains one statement:

```
PRINT #2; ACCOUNT.NO%,NAME$,AMOUNT
```

%CHAIN DIRECTIVE

The %CHAIN directive is used when a program transfers execution to another program using the CHAIN statement. (See Chapter 8.) The %CHAIN directive instructs the *first* program to determine what the maximum size of the following programs will be. In other words, the %CHAIN directive identifies the program that provides the maximum size of the constant, code, data, and variable areas used by all subsequent programs which it chains to. When a program is compiled, the values of the constant, code, data, and variable areas print on the console. (See Figure 16-1.) After all programs that will be chained together have been compiled, the largest value of each area is used in the %CHAIN directive.

TRACING EXECUTION OF A CBASIC PROGRAM

When a CBASIC program is compiled with the E toggle (described earlier), the programmer may trace the execution of each line in the program. The following command will execute the program TEST.INT and trace the execution:

```
CRUN2 TEST TRACE
```

```
A>CRUN2 TEST TRACE

CRUN VER 2.07
AT LINE 0002
AT LINE 0003
AT LINE 0004
 4.5
AT LINE 0006
```

Figure 16-5. Sample Run of TEST.BAS, With TRACE Enabled

The output produced is shown in Figure 16-5.

Remember that the trace command can only be used if the program was compiled with the E toggle.

Selective tracing can be specified by providing a range of line numbers. For example:

CRUN2 TEST TRACE 1,2

will trace all executions of lines 1 through 2. The command

CRUN2 TEST TRACE 3

will trace execution of line 3 and any line beyond line 3.

A

CBASIC Error Messages and Codes

TWO-LETTER ERROR CODES

IF YOU ARE LOOKING for the meaning of a two-letter CBASIC error code, see Table A-1 for an alphabetic summary of CBASIC error codes. This summary contains compiler and run-time error codes in the same table.

After the two-letter code in the leftmost column of Table A-1, you will see the letter C (meaning compiler error), R (meaning run-time error), or R^W (indicating a run-time warning). Compiler errors do not stop compilation of a CBASIC program. Run-time warnings provide information; they inform you that CBASIC took certain action to correct an emergent mistake. The next column to the right explains the error code, and the next column offers corrective actions to rectify the error and guard against its recurrence.

The compiler error codes appear in the format:

ERROR XX IN LINE nnnn AT POSITION nnn

The error message containing the two-letter code will appear on the line immediately after the error itself, indicating in which line and exactly where on the line the error occurred. CBASIC will not generate a complete .INT file if compiler error codes were generated. Re-edit the incorrect statement(s) and compile the program again.

Run-time error codes can appear two ways:

ERROR XX

By itself, this error message is not very helpful. If you compile a CBASIC program with the $E toggle (see Chapter 16), you will receive a more informative message if an error occurs:

ERROR XX IN LINE nnnn AT POSITION nn

The line displayed in the error message is the line number which the compiler used, not a CBASIC statement number. To isolate the statement which caused the error, look at the latest compiler listing of the program or re-compile the program and observe which statement resides at the line number referenced in the error message. The $E toggle has a disadvantage: programs using the $E toggle will take up more memory when you run the program.

CBASIC COMPILER ERROR MESSAGES

These messages will occur when compiling a CBASIC program. Their explanations follow.

NO SOURCE FILE: *filename*. BAS

The compiler could not locate a source file used in either a CBASIC command or an INCLUDE directive.

OUT OF DISK SPACE

The compiler has run out of disk space while attempting to write either the .INT file or the .LST file.

OUT OF DIRECTORY SPACE

The compiler has run out of directory space while attempting to create or extend a file.

DISK ERROR

A disk error occurred while trying to read or write to a disk file.

PROGRAM CONTAINS n UNMATCHED FOR STATEMENT(S)

There are n FOR statements for which a NEXT could not be found.

PROGRAM CONTAINS n UNMATCHED WHILE STATEMENT(S)

There are n WHILE statements for which a WEND could not be found.

PROGRAM CONTAINS 1 UNMATCHED DEF STATEMENT

A multiple-line function was not terminated with an FEND statement. This may cause other errors in the program.

WARNING INVALID CHARACTER IGNORED

The previous line contained an invalid ASCII character. The character is ignored by the compiler. A question mark is printed in its place.

INCLUDE NESTING TOO DEEP NEAR LINE n

An include statement near line n in the source program exceeds the maximum level of nesting of source files.

CBASIC RUN-TIME ERROR MESSAGES

NO INTERMEDIATE FILE

A file name was not specified after CRUN2, or no file of type INT and the specified file name was found on the disk.

IMPROPER INPUT — REENTER

This message occurs when the fields entered from the console do not match the fields specified in the INPUT statement. This can occur when field types do not match or the number of fields entered is different from the number of fields specified. Following this message all values required by the input statement must be reentered.

Table A-1. Summary of CBASIC Error Codes

Code	Type	Explanation	Corrective action for program
AC	R	The ASC function attempted to evaluate a null string.	Test for a zero string length before using ASC.
BF	C	A GOTO or GOSUB branched to a line number within a multiple-line function, from outside the function definition.	GOTOs or GOSUBs are allowed only within multiple-line functions from other statements within the function. Change the GOTO or GOSUB statement, or the function itself.
BN	C	An invalid numeric constant was used; e.g., 1055B, 9.0E99, etc.	The constant must be within the range of valid CBASIC numbers, and the notation (binary, decimal, or hex) must be appropriate to the value used.
BN	R	An OPEN or CREATE statement specified a BUFF value less than 1 or greater than 52.	Test for improper BUFF values before executing the statement, or correct the expression after BUFF.
CC	R	The CHAIN statement loaded a program which has a larger code area than the main program.	Re compile the main program with corrected sizes in the %CHAIN compiler directive.
CD	R	The CHAIN statement loaded a program which has a larger data area than the main program.	See CC.
CE	R	A CP/M file error occurred while closing a disk file.	Inspect the file using a text editor. Restore file from backup if necessary.
CF	R	Same as CC and CD errors; the chained program's constant area is too large.	See CC.
CI	C	A %INCLUDE compiler directive specified an invalid file name.	The file name must be unambiguous (that is, no * or ? characters).
CP	R	The chained program's variable storage area is too large; same as CC, CD, and CF errors.	See CC.
CS	C	A COMMON statement was not the first executable statement in a program.	Relocate the COMMON statement at the beginning of the program.
CS	R	A chained program contains a SAVEMEM statement which does not reserve the same amount of memory specified in a main program's SAVEMEM statement.	Make sure that the main program and all programs it chains to use the same integer constant in the SAVEMEM statement.
CU	R	A CLOSE statement executed for a file which was not open at the time.	Delete the CLOSE statement or check file logic in the program.
CV	C	The subscript used for an array variable is incorrect in a COMMON statement.	Change the COMMON statement. Only one constant may be used when declaring common array variables.
DF	R	An OPEN or CREATE statement was executed for a file which is already open.	The file number could be wrong. If not, make sure that the file is closed first. IF END# does not resolve this error.
DL	C	The program contains duplicate line numbers.	Every line number must be different. Change the program with a unique line number, or delete the duplicate line number if it is not referenced by the program.

Table A-1. Summary of CBASIC Error Codes (Continued)

Code	Type	Explanation	Corrective action for program
DP	C	A DIM statement appears more than once for the same array variable.	Eliminate the duplicate DIM statement(s). If you use DIM to initialize an array, locate the DIM statement in a function and call the function to initialize this or other arrays.
DU	R	DELETE occurred for a file which was not open at the time.	Check for CLOSE statements which precede DELETE for the file number.
DW	R	A CP/M disk write error occurred. Either the directory is full or no more space is available on the disk.	Delete or move some disk files to allow more room.
DZ	R^w	A number was divided by zero.	CBASIC sets the result to the largest valid number (integers 32767, real numbers 9.9E62).
EF	R	A READ# statement executed for a file which is already past the end of file; no IF END# statement exists for that file.	Place an IF END# statement in the program in order to trap all end-of-file errors.
ER	R	A PRINT# statement for a randomly organized file would send out data longer than the record length specified in the file's OPEN, CREATE, or FILE statement.	Recalculate correct record length for the OPEN statement or correct the PRINT# which caused the error.
FD	C	More than one DEF FN statement, with the same function name, was used in a program.	Make sure all function names are unique. Change at least one function name.
FE	C	A FOR/NEXT statement uses a terminal value expression which is not the same data type as the index variable.	Change the terminal value expression to the same data type as the index variable.
FI	C	An invalid variable name was used as a FOR/NEXT index variable.	Make sure the variable is a simple integer or real numeric variable (i.e., not an array variable or a string).
FL	R^w	READ#LINE attempted to read a data record longer than 255 bytes.	CBASIC truncates the string to the first 255 characters.
FN	C	A function reference contains an incorrect number of parameters in parentheses.	Each DEF FN statement parameter list must have a matching number of parameters in every function reference.
FP	C	A function reference contains parameters of a data type which does not match the function definition parameters.	Change the function reference parameters to the correct data type.
FR	R	The RENAME function used an existing file name in the first parameter.	Delete the file or correct the first RENAME parameter.
FT	R	A FILE statement executed when 20 files were already open.	Close any unused files before executing the FILE statement.
FU	C	A function was referenced before it was defined.	Place the function definition before its first reference in the program.
FU	R	A READ# or PRINT# statement was executed for a file which is not open.	Open the file before attempting to read it or write to it.

Table A-1. Summary of CBASIC Error Codes (Continued)

Code	Type	Explanation	Corrective action for program
IE	C	An IF statement was used to test the logical value of a string (e.g., IF A$ THEN...).	Change the statement to a comparison (e.g., IF A$ = '' '' THEN...).
IF	C	A FILE statement used a numeric variable name instead of a string variable name.	Change the FILE statement for the proper variable name.
IF	R	An invalid character exists in a disk file name; either *, ?, or : was used incorrectly.	Eliminate the incorrect characters.
IP	C	An INPUT statement has no quotes around the prompt string.	Make sure that double quotes ('') surround the prompt string.
IR	R	A READ# or PRINT# statement for a randomly organized file specified a record number less than 1.	Check the expression used to calculate the record number.
IS	C	An array variable was used in a program before it was dimensioned.	Place the DIM statement before the array variable's first use in the program.
IT	C	A compiler directive is incorrect.	An incorrect directive or parameter could be the cause. Check both. See Chapter 16.
IU	C	An array variable was used without subscripts.	Add the subscript or change the variable name.
IV	R	A CBASIC .INT file was compiled with CBASIC Version 1.	Re-compile the source program under CBASIC Version 2.
IX	R	An FEND statement executed in a multiple-line function.	All multiple-line functions use the RETURN statement to exit the function. Change the function definition.
LN	R^w	A LOG function's argument was less than or equal to 0.	The function returns the value of the argument without taking its LOG.
LW	R	An LPRINTER statement executed with an invalid WIDTH parameter.	The WIDTH parameter value cannot be greater than 132 or less than 0.
ME	R	The disk directory became full when creating a file for opening a new file extent.	Delete unused files to allow for more directory space.
MF	C	A string expression was used when a numeric expression was expected.	Change the expression to evaluate to a number.
MM	C	CBASIC could not compile a statement which used both strings and numeric data.	Convert strings to numeric data using VAL or ASC; or, convert numeric data to strings using STR$ or CHR$.
MP	R	The MATCH function contained a zero or negative parameter for the starting character position.	Test for a zero value before using MATCH, or correct the expression in the third MATCH parameter.
MS	C	A numeric expression was used in a CBASIC statement when a string expression was expected.	Change the expression to evaluate to a string.
ND	C	The compiler encountered an FEND statement which did not have a corresponding DEF FN statement.	Remove the FEND or insert the DEF FN. Also, if the DEF FN specified a single-line function, no FEND statement is necessary.

Table A-1. Summary of CBASIC Error Codes (Continued)

Code	Type	Explanation	Corrective action for program
NE	R^w	Exponentiation (^ operation) was used on a negative number.	CBASIC takes the absolute value of the negative number, then exponentiates the number.
NF	R	A file number less than 1 or more than 20 was used in an OPEN, CREATE, READ#, PRINT#, CLOSE, or DELETE statement.	Replace the file number or correct the expression which evaluates to the file number.
NI	C	A NEXT statement occurs for the wrong index variable in a FOR/NEXT loop.	Nested FOR/NEXT loops should not cross. Define loops only when they end inside other FOR/NEXT loops. See Chapter 7 for explanation.
NM	R	Not enough memory is available to execute the program.	Generate a larger CP/M system (see *CP/M System Alteration Guide* from Digital Research, or *Osborne CP/M User's Guide* from Osborne/McGraw-Hill). You may have to divide the program into overlays. See Chapter 8 for more information.
NN	R	A PRINT USING statement has a numeric format string, but there are no numeric variables to print.	Place a numeric variable at the end of the PRINT USING statement.
NS	R	A PRINT USING statement has a format string which specifies string data, but there are no string data items to print.	Correct the format string, or correct the variable list.
NU	C	A NEXT statement does not have a matching FOR statement.	Delete the FOR statement or the NEXT statement.
OD	R	A READ statement executed when there was no DATA statement to read from; it also occurs if all data have been read.	Add a DATA statement, or use RESTORE to place the pointer to the beginning of the data list.
OE	R	An OPEN statement was executed for a nonexistent file, and no IF END# was executed for that file number.	Place an IF END# statement before the OPEN statement; also check for an incorrect diskette drive assignment in the file name.
OF	C	A GOTO statement inside a multiple-line function branches outside the function definition.	GOTO statements within a multiple-line function definition are allowed only if they branch elsewhere within the function. Use RETURN to exit functions.
OF	R^w	Overflow occurred during a calculation.	The calculation's result is set to the largest valid CBASIC number.
OI	R	An ON GOSUB or ON GOTO contains a selector which has a zero value, or the selector is greater than the number of statements to branch to.	Make sure the selector is greater than zero but not greater than the number of statements it can possibly branch to.
OM	R	The program ran out of memory during execution.	Break the program up into overlays. See Chapter 8.
OO	C	More than 25 ON GOTO or ON GOSUB statements exist in the program.	Use other logical tests (IF-THEN, WHILE/WEND) as substitutes.
PM	C	More than one DEF FN statement was used in a multiple-line function definition.	Move the function outside the function it is currently in.

Table A-1. Summary of CBASIC Error Codes (Continued)

Code	Type	Explanation	Corrective action for program
QE	R	A PRINT# statement attempted to write a data record which contains double-quote characters inside a string.	A double quote (") is a string delimiter. Only PRINT USING# allows quotes to appear within strings.
RB	R	A random-access READ# or PRINT# executed for a file with a BUFF value greater than 1.	The random form of READ# and PRINT# (i.e., with a specified record number) is not allowed for files opened with data buffers more than 128 bytes long.
RE	R	While executing a READ# statement for a file with fixed record lengths, the end of a record was reached unexpectedly.	Check the expression after RECL in the OPEN statement, or check the expression in parentheses after FILE (if FILE was used to open the file). Make sure it is correct. See Chapter 11 for information on calculating record lengths.
RG	R	A RETURN statement executed without a corresponding GOSUB.	Check program logic; correct any GOTO which should actually be a GOSUB.
RU	R	A random-access READ# or PRINT# statement executed for a file which was opened as a sequential file.	Include the record length parameter when opening the file.
SB	R	The subscript used for an array variable is greater than the highest subscript defined in that variable's DIM statement.	Change the DIM statement for a larger array, or correct the subscript which caused the error.
SE	C	The compiler encountered a syntax error; either a key word was misspelled or a statment has incorrect parameters.	See Chapters 14 and 15 for detailed descriptions of CBASIC statement and function syntax.
SL	R	Concatenation resulted in a string longer than 255 bytes.	Check the string's length before concatenating.
SN	C	An array variable used in a program does not have the same dimension as its DIM statement.	Change the subscripts in the array variable.
SO	E	CBASIC could not find a file to load as specified in the SAVEMEM statement.	Re-compile the program with the correct file name, or place the file on the correct disk.
SQ	R^w	The SQR function was used for a negative number.	CBASIC takes the square root of the absolute value of the number instead.
SS	R	The second parameter of the MID$ function is less than or equal to 0.	Test for a zero value before using MID$, or correct the expression to yield a non-zero value.
TF	R	More than 20 files were active at one time.	This error should not occur. It is possible if RENAME was used while 20 files were already active. Keep unused files closed.
TL	R	A TAB function parameter is less than 1 or greater than the current line width.	Correct the expression in the TAB function.
TO	C	The program is too large to be compiled, given available memory.	See corrective action for error code NM.

Table A-1. Summary of CBASIC Error Codes (Continued)

Code	Type	Explanation	Corrective action for program
UL	C	A GOTO or GOSUB referenced a line which is not in the program.	Check for typographical errors, or number the statement to branch to.
UN	R	An invalid format string was used in a PRINT USING statement.	The string could be null, or a backslash (\) character was the last character in the format string. See Chapter 10 for more information on format strings.
US	C	A string did not end with a double quote character.	Place a double quote character at the end of the string.
VO	C	Variable name was too long for one statement.	This error should not occur. Compiler Systems, Inc., asks CBASIC users encountering this error to send a copy of the progam statement to them.
WE	C	The expression after WHILE could not be evaluated because it is not a numeric value, nor is it a logical value.	This occurs when strings are used as logical values, e.g., WHILE A$. In this case, change the statement to WHILE LEN(A$). This will generate a logical (numeric) value which WHILE can evaluate.
WR	R	A sequential-format PRINT# statement was used with a file having a fixed record length; this causes an error if the file was not read completely to the end before writing occurred.	Advance to the end of a random-access file before writing data to it with sequential-format PRINT# statements.
WU	C	A WEND statement does not have a corresponding WHILE statement.	Delete the WEND statement or insert a proper WHILE statement.

B
Conversion Tables

THIS APPENDIX CONTAINS the following reference table:

- Hexadecimal-Decimal Integer Conversion

HEXADECIMAL-DECIMAL INTEGER CONVERSION

The table below provides for direct conversions between hexa-decimal integers in the range 0−FFF and decimal integers in the range 0−4095. For conversion of larger integers, the table values may be added to the following figures:

Hexadecimal	Decimal	Hexadecimal	Decimal
01 000	4 096	20 000	131 072
02 000	8 192	30 000	196 608
03 000	12 288	40 000	262 144
04 000	16 384	50 000	327 680
05 000	20 480	60 000	393 216
06 000	24 576	70 000	458 752
07 000	28 672	80 000	524 288
08 000	32 768	90 000	589 824
09 000	36 864	A0 000	655 360
0A 000	40 960	B0 000	720 896
0B 000	45 056	C0 000	786 432
0C 000	49 152	D0 000	851 968
0D 000	53 248	E0 000	917 504
0E 000	57 344	F0 000	983 040
0F 000	61 440	100 000	1 048 576
10 000	65 536	200 000	2 097 152
11 000	69 632	300 000	3 145 728
12 000	73 728	400 000	4 194 304
13 000	77 824	500 000	5 242 880
14 000	81 920	600 000	6 291 456
15 000	86 016	700 000	7 340 032
16 000	90 112	800 000	8 388 608
17 000	94 208	900 000	9 437 184
18 000	98 304	A00 000	10 485 760
19 000	102 400	B00 000	11 534 336
1A 000	106 496	C00 000	12 582 912
1B 000	110 592	D00 000	13 631 488
1C 000	114 688	E00 000	14 680 064
1D 000	118 784	F00 000	15 728 640
1E 000	122 880	1 000 000	16 777 216
1F 000	126 976	2 000 000	33 554 432

Hexadecimal fractions may be converted to decimal fractions as follows:

1. Express the hexadecimal fraction as an integer times 16^{-n}, where n is the number of significant hexadecimal places to the right of the hexadecimal point.

$$0. CA9BF3_{16} = CA9 BF3_{16} \times 16^{-6}$$

2. Find the decimal equivalent of the hexadecimal integer

$$CA9 BF3_{16} = 13 278 195_{10}$$

3. Multiply the decimal equivalent by 16^{-n}

$$\begin{array}{r} 13 278 195 \\ \times\ 596 046 448 \times 10^{-16} \\ \hline 0.791 442 096_{10} \end{array}$$

Decimal fractions may be converted to hexadecimal fractions by successively multiplying the decimal fraction by 16_{10}. After each multiplication, the integer portion is removed to form a hexadecimal fraction by building to the right of the hexadecimal point. However, since decimal arithmetic is used in this conversion, the integer portion of each product must be converted to hexadecimal numbers.

Example: Convert 0.895_{10} to its hexadecimal equivalent

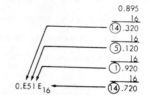

	0	1	2	3	4	5	6	7	8	9	A	B	C	D	E	F
00	0000	0001	0002	0003	0004	0005	0006	0007	0008	0009	0010	0011	0012	0013	0014	0015
01	0016	0017	0018	0019	0020	0021	0022	0023	0024	0025	0026	0027	0028	0029	0030	0031
02	0032	0033	0034	0035	0036	0037	0038	0039	0040	0041	0042	0043	0044	0045	0046	0047
03	0048	0049	0050	0051	0052	0053	0054	0055	0056	0057	0058	0059	0060	0061	0062	0063
04	0064	0065	0066	0067	0068	0069	0070	0071	0072	0073	0074	0075	0076	0077	0078	0079
05	0080	0081	0082	0083	0084	0085	0086	0087	0088	0089	0090	0091	0092	0093	0094	0095
06	0096	0097	0098	0099	0100	0101	0102	0103	0104	0105	0106	0107	0108	0109	0110	0111
07	0112	0113	0114	0115	0116	0117	0118	0119	0120	0121	0122	0123	0124	0125	0126	0127
08	0128	0129	0130	0131	0132	0133	0134	0135	0136	0137	0138	0139	0140	0141	0142	0143
09	0144	0145	0146	0147	0148	0149	0150	0151	0152	0153	0154	0155	0156	0157	0158	0159
0A	0160	0161	0162	0163	0164	0165	0166	0167	0168	0169	0170	0171	0172	0173	0174	0175
0B	0176	0177	0178	0179	0180	0181	0182	0183	0184	0185	0186	0187	0188	0189	0190	0191
0C	0192	0193	0194	0195	0196	0197	0198	0199	0200	0201	0202	0203	0204	0205	0206	0207
0D	0208	0209	0210	0211	0212	0213	0214	0215	0216	0217	0218	0219	0220	0221	0222	0223
0E	0224	0225	0226	0227	0228	0229	0230	0231	0232	0233	0234	0235	0236	0237	0238	0239
0F	0240	0241	0242	0243	0244	0245	0246	0247	0248	0249	0250	0251	0252	0253	0254	0255

HEXADECIMAL-DECIMAL INTEGER CONVERSION (Continued)

	0	1	2	3	4	5	6	7	8	9	A	B	C	D	E	F
10	0256	0257	0258	0259	0260	0261	0262	0263	0264	0265	0266	0267	0268	0269	0270	0271
11	0272	0273	0274	0275	0276	0277	0278	0279	0280	0281	0282	0283	0284	0285	0286	0287
12	0288	0289	0290	0291	0292	0293	0294	0295	0296	0297	0298	0299	0300	0301	0302	0303
13	0304	0305	0306	0307	0308	0309	0310	0311	0312	0313	0314	0315	0316	0317	0318	0319
14	0320	0321	0322	0323	0324	0325	0326	0327	0328	0329	0330	0331	0332	0333	0334	0335
15	0336	0337	0338	0339	0340	0341	0342	0343	0344	0345	0346	0347	0348	0349	0350	0351
16	0352	0353	0354	0355	0356	0357	0358	0359	0360	0361	0362	0363	0364	0365	0366	0367
17	0368	0369	0370	0371	0372	0373	0374	0375	0376	0377	0378	0379	0380	0381	0382	0383
18	0384	0385	0386	0387	0388	0389	0390	0391	0392	0393	0394	0395	0396	0397	0398	0399
19	0400	0401	0402	0403	0404	0405	0406	0407	0408	0409	0410	0411	0412	0413	0414	0415
1A	0416	0417	0418	0419	0420	0421	0422	0423	0424	0425	0426	0427	0428	0429	0430	0431
1B	0432	0433	0434	0435	0436	0437	0438	0439	0440	0441	0442	0443	0444	0445	0446	0447
1C	0448	0449	0450	0451	0452	0453	0454	0455	0456	0457	0458	0459	0460	0461	0462	0463
1D	0464	0465	0466	0467	0468	0469	0470	0471	0472	0473	0474	0475	0476	0477	0478	0479
1E	0480	0481	0482	0483	0484	0485	0486	0487	0488	0489	0490	0491	0492	0493	0494	0495
1F	0496	0497	0498	0499	0500	0501	0502	0503	0504	0505	0506	0507	0508	0509	0510	0511
20	0512	0513	0514	0515	0516	0517	0518	0519	0520	0521	0522	0523	0524	0525	0526	0527
21	0528	0529	0530	0531	0532	0533	0534	0535	0536	0537	0538	0539	0540	0541	0542	0543
22	0544	0545	0546	0547	0548	0549	0550	0551	0552	0553	0554	0555	0556	0557	0558	0559
23	0560	0561	0562	0563	0564	0565	0566	0567	0568	0569	0570	0571	0572	0573	0574	0575
24	0576	0577	0578	0579	0580	0581	0582	0583	0584	0585	0586	0587	0588	0589	0590	0591
25	0592	0593	0594	0595	0596	0597	0598	0599	0600	0601	0602	0603	0604	0605	0606	0607
26	0608	0609	0610	0611	0612	0613	0614	0615	0616	0617	0618	0619	0620	0621	0622	0623
27	0624	0625	0626	0627	0628	0629	0630	0631	0632	0633	0634	0635	0636	0637	0638	0639
28	0640	0641	0642	0643	0644	0645	0646	0647	0648	0649	0650	0651	0652	0653	0654	0655
29	0656	0657	0658	0659	0660	0661	0662	0663	0664	0665	0666	0667	0668	0669	0670	0671
2A	0672	0673	0674	0675	0676	0677	0678	0679	0680	0681	0682	0683	0684	0685	0686	0687
2B	0688	0689	0690	0691	0692	0693	0694	0695	0696	0697	0698	0699	0700	0701	0702	0703
2C	0704	0705	0706	0707	0708	0709	0710	0711	0712	0713	0714	0715	0716	0717	0718	0719
2D	0720	0721	0722	0723	0724	0725	0726	0727	0728	0729	0730	0731	0732	0733	0734	0735
2E	0736	0737	0738	0739	0740	0741	0742	0743	0744	0745	0746	0747	0748	0749	0750	0751
2F	0752	0753	0754	0755	0756	0757	0758	0759	0760	0761	0762	0763	0764	0765	0766	0767
30	0768	0769	0770	0771	0772	0773	0774	0775	0776	0777	0778	0779	0780	0781	0782	0783
31	0784	0785	0786	0787	0788	0789	0790	0791	0792	0793	0794	0795	0796	0797	0798	0799
32	0800	0801	0802	0803	0804	0805	0806	0807	0808	0809	0810	0811	0812	0813	0814	0815
33	0816	0817	0818	0819	0820	0821	0822	0823	0824	0825	0826	0827	0828	0829	0830	0631
34	0832	0833	0834	0835	0836	0837	0838	0839	0840	0841	0842	0843	0844	0845	0846	0847
35	0848	0849	0850	0851	0852	0853	0854	0855	0856	0857	0858	0859	0860	0861	0862	0863
36	0864	0865	0866	0867	0868	0869	0870	0871	0872	0873	0874	0875	0876	0877	0878	0879
37	0880	0881	0882	0883	0884	0885	0886	0887	0888	0889	0890	0891	0892	0893	0894	0895
38	0896	0897	0898	0899	0900	0901	0902	0903	0904	0905	0906	0907	0908	0909	0910	0911
39	0912	0913	0914	0915	0916	0917	0918	0919	0920	0921	0922	0923	0924	0925	0926	0927
3A	0928	0929	0930	0931	0932	0933	0934	0935	0936	0937	0938	0939	0940	0941	0942	0943
3B	0944	0945	0946	0947	0948	0949	0950	0951	0952	0953	0954	0955	0956	0957	0958	0959
3C	0960	0961	0962	0963	0964	0965	0966	0967	0968	0969	0970	0971	0972	0973	0974	0975
3D	0976	0977	0978	0979	0980	0981	0982	0983	0984	0985	0986	0987	0988	0989	0990	0991
3E	0992	0993	0994	0995	0996	0997	0998	0999	1000	1001	1002	1003	1004	1005	1006	1007
3F	1008	1009	1010	1011	1012	1013	1014	1015	1016	1017	1018	1019	1020	1021	1022	1023

HEXADECIMAL-DECIMAL INTEGER CONVERSION (Continued)

	0	1	2	3	4	5	6	7	8	9	A	B	C	D	E	F
40	1024	1025	1026	1027	1028	1029	1030	1031	1032	1033	1034	1035	1036	1037	1038	1039
41	1040	1041	1042	1043	1044	1045	1046	1047	1048	1049	1050	1051	1052	1053	1054	1055
42	1056	1057	1058	1059	1060	1061	1062	1063	1064	1065	1066	1067	1068	1069	1070	1071
43	1072	1073	1074	1075	1076	1077	1078	1079	1080	1081	1082	1083	1084	1085	1086	1087
44	1088	1089	1090	1091	1092	1093	1094	1095	1096	1097	1098	1099	1100	1101	1102	1103
45	1104	1105	1106	1107	1108	1109	1110	1111	1112	1113	1114	1115	1116	1117	1118	1119
46	1120	1121	1122	1123	1124	1125	1126	1127	1128	1129	1130	1131	1132	1133	1134	1135
47	1136	1137	1138	1139	1140	1141	1142	1143	1144	1145	1146	1147	1148	1149	1150	1151
48	1152	1153	1154	1155	1156	1157	1158	1159	1160	1161	1162	1163	1164	1165	1166	1167
49	1168	1169	1170	1171	1172	1173	1174	1175	1176	1177	1178	1179	1180	1181	1182	1183
4A	1184	1185	1186	1187	1188	1189	1190	1191	1192	1193	1194	1195	1196	1197	1198	1199
4B	1200	1201	1202	1203	1204	1205	1206	1207	1208	1209	1210	1211	1212	1213	1214	1215
4C	1216	1217	1218	1219	1220	1221	1222	1223	1224	1225	1226	1227	1228	1229	1230	1231
4C	1232	1233	1234	1235	1236	1237	1238	1239	1240	1241	1242	1243	1244	1245	1246	1247
4E	1248	1249	1250	1251	1252	1253	1254	1255	1256	1257	1258	1259	1260	1261	1262	1263
4F	1264	1265	1266	1267	1268	1269	1270	1271	1272	1273	1274	1275	1276	1277	1278	1279
50	1280	1281	1282	1283	1284	1285	1286	1287	1288	1289	1290	1291	1292	1293	1294	1295
51	1296	1297	1298	1299	1300	1301	1302	1303	1304	1305	1306	1307	1308	1309	1310	1311
52	1312	1313	1314	1315	1316	1317	1318	1319	1320	1321	1322	1323	1324	1325	1326	1327
53	1328	1329	1330	1331	1332	1333	1334	1335	1336	1337	1338	1339	1340	1341	1342	1343
54	1344	1345	1346	1347	1348	1349	1350	1351	1352	1353	1354	1355	1356	1357	1358	1359
55	1360	1361	1362	1363	1364	1365	1366	1367	1368	1369	1370	1371	1372	1373	1374	1375
56	1376	1377	1378	1379	1380	1381	1382	1383	1384	1385	1386	1387	1388	1389	1390	1391
57	1392	1393	1394	1395	1396	1397	1398	1399	1400	1401	1402	1403	1404	1405	1406	1407
58	1408	1409	1410	1411	1412	1413	1414	1415	1416	1417	1418	1419	1420	1421	1422	1423
59	1424	1425	1426	1427	1428	1429	1430	1431	1432	1433	1434	1435	1436	1437	1438	1439
5A	1440	1441	1442	1443	1444	1445	1446	1447	1448	1449	1450	1451	1452	1453	1454	1455
5B	1456	1457	1458	1459	1460	1461	1462	1463	1464	1465	1466	1467	1468	1469	1470	1471
5C	1472	1473	1474	1475	1476	1477	1478	1479	1480	1481	1482	1483	1484	1485	1486	1487
5D	1488	1489	1490	1491	1492	1493	1494	1495	1496	1497	1498	1499	1500	1501	1502	1503
5E	1504	1505	1506	1507	1508	1509	1510	1511	1512	1513	1514	1515	1516	1517	1518	1519
5F	1520	1521	1522	1523	1524	1525	1526	1527	1528	1529	1530	1531	1532	1533	1534	1535
60	1536	1537	1538	1539	1540	1541	1542	1543	1544	1545	1546	1547	1548	1549	1550	1551
61	1552	1553	1554	1555	1556	1557	1558	1559	1560	1561	1562	1563	1564	1565	1566	1567
62	1568	1569	1570	1571	1572	1573	1574	1575	1576	1577	1578	1579	1580	1581	1582	1583
63	1584	1585	1586	1587	1588	1589	1590	1591	1592	1593	1594	1595	1596	1597	1598	1599
64	1600	1601	1602	1603	1604	1605	1606	1607	1608	1609	1610	1611	1612	1613	1614	1615
65	1616	1617	1618	1619	1620	1621	1622	1623	1624	1625	1626	1627	1628	1629	1630	1631
66	1632	1633	1634	1635	1636	1637	1638	1639	1640	1641	1642	1643	1644	1645	1646	1647
67	1648	1649	1650	1651	1652	1653	1654	1655	1656	1657	1658	1659	1660	1661	1562	1663
68	1664	1665	1666	1667	1668	1669	1670	1671	1672	1673	1674	1675	1676	1677	1678	1679
69	1680	1681	1682	1683	1684	1685	1686	1687	1688	1689	1690	1691	1692	1693	1694	1695
6A	1696	1697	1698	1699	1700	1701	1702	1703	1704	1705	1706	1707	1708	1709	1710	1711
6B	1712	1713	1714	1715	1716	1717	1718	1719	1720	1721	1722	1723	1724	1725	1726	1727
6C	1728	1729	1730	1731	1732	1733	1734	1735	1736	1737	1738	1739	1740	1741	1742	1743
6D	1744	1745	1746	1747	1748	1749	1750	1751	1752	1753	1754	1755	1756	1757	1758	1759
6E	1760	1761	1762	1763	1764	1765	1766	1767	1768	1769	1770	1771	1772	1773	1774	1775
6F	1776	1777	1778	1779	1780	1781	1782	1783	1784	1785	1786	1787	1788	1789	1790	1791

HEXADECIMAL-DECIMAL INTEGER CONVERSION (Continued)

	0	1	2	3	4	5	6	7	8	9	A	B	C	D	E	F
70	1792	1793	1794	1795	1796	1797	1798	1799	1800	1801	1802	1803	1804	1805	1806	1807
71	1808	1809	1810	1811	1812	1813	1814	1815	1816	1817	1818	1819	1820	1821	1822	1823
72	1824	1825	1826	1827	1828	1829	1830	1831	1832	1833	1834	1835	1836	1837	1838	1839
73	1840	1841	1842	1843	1844	1845	1846	1847	1848	1849	1850	1851	1852	1853	1854	1855
74	1856	1857	1858	1859	1860	1861	1862	1863	1864	1865	1866	1867	1868	1869	1870	1871
75	1872	1873	1874	1875	1876	1877	1878	1879	1880	1881	1882	1883	1884	1885	1886	1887
76	1888	1889	1890	1891	1892	1893	1894	1895	1896	1897	1898	1899	1900	1901	1902	1903
77	1904	1905	1906	1907	1908	1909	1910	1911	1912	1913	1914	1915	1916	1917	1918	1919
78	1920	1921	1922	1923	1924	1925	1926	1927	1928	1929	1930	1931	1932	1933	1934	1935
79	1936	1937	1938	1939	1940	1941	1942	1943	1944	1945	1946	1947	1948	1949	1950	1951
7A	1952	1953	1954	1955	1956	1957	1958	1959	1960	1961	1962	1963	1964	1965	1966	1967
7B	1968	1969	1970	1971	1972	1973	1974	1975	1976	1977	1978	1979	1980	1981	1982	1983
7C	1984	1985	1986	1987	1988	1989	1990	1991	1992	1993	1994	1995	1996	1997	1998	1999
7D	2000	2001	2002	2003	2004	2005	2006	2007	2008	2009	2010	2011	2012	2013	2014	2015
7E	2016	2017	2018	2019	2020	2021	2022	2023	2024	2025	2026	2027	2028	2029	2030	2031
7F	2032	2033	2034	2035	2036	2037	2038	2039	2040	2041	2042	2043	2044	2045	2046	2047
80	2048	2049	2050	2051	2052	2053	2054	2055	2056	2057	2058	2059	2060	2061	2062	2063
81	2064	2065	2066	2067	2068	2069	2070	2071	2072	2073	2074	2075	2076	2077	2078	2079
82	2080	2081	2082	2083	2084	2085	2086	2087	2088	2089	2090	2091	2092	2093	2094	2095
83	2096	2097	2098	2099	2100	2101	2102	2103	2104	2105	2106	2107	2108	2109	2110	2111
84	2112	2113	2114	2115	2116	2117	2118	2119	2120	2121	2122	2123	2124	2125	2126	2127
85	2128	2129	2130	2131	2132	2133	2134	2135	2136	2137	2138	2139	2140	2141	2142	2143
86	2144	2145	2146	2147	2148	2149	2150	2151	2152	2153	2154	2155	2156	2157	2158	2159
87	2160	2161	2162	2163	2164	2165	2166	2167	2168	2169	2170	2171	2172	2173	2174	2175
88	2176	2177	2178	2179	2180	2181	2182	2183	2184	2185	2186	2187	2188	2189	2190	2191
89	2192	2193	2194	2195	2196	2197	2198	2199	2200	2201	2202	2203	2204	2205	2206	2207
8A	2208	2209	2210	2211	2212	2213	2214	2215	2216	2217	2218	2219	2220	2221	2222	2223
8B	2224	2225	2226	2227	2228	2229	2230	2231	2232	2233	2234	2235	2236	2237	2238	2239
8C	2240	2241	2242	2243	2244	2245	2246	2247	2248	2249	2250	2251	2252	2253	2254	2255
8D	2256	2257	2258	2259	2260	2261	2262	2263	2264	2265	2266	2267	2268	2269	2270	2271
8E	2272	2273	2274	2275	2276	2277	2278	2279	2280	2281	2282	2283	2284	2285	2286	2287
8F	2288	2289	2290	2291	2292	2293	2294	2295	2296	2297	2298	2299	2300	2301	2302	2303
90	2304	2305	2306	2307	2308	2309	2310	2311	2312	2313	2314	2315	2316	2317	2318	2319
91	2320	2321	2322	2323	2324	2325	2326	2327	2328	2329	2330	2331	2332	2333	2334	2335
92	2336	2337	2338	2339	2340	2341	2342	2343	2344	2345	2346	2347	2348	2349	2350	2351
93	2352	2353	2354	2355	2356	2357	2358	2359	2360	2361	2362	2363	2364	2365	2366	2367
94	2368	2369	2370	2371	2372	2373	2374	2375	2376	2377	2378	2379	2380	2381	2382	2383
95	2384	2385	2386	2387	2388	2389	2390	2391	2392	2393	2394	2395	2396	2397	2398	2399
96	2400	2401	2402	2403	2404	2405	2406	2407	2408	2409	2410	2411	2412	2413	2414	2415
97	2416	2417	2418	2419	2420	2421	2422	2423	2424	2425	2426	2427	2428	2429	2430	2431
98	2432	2433	2434	2435	2436	2437	2438	2439	2440	2441	2442	2443	2444	2445	2446	2447
99	2448	2449	2450	2451	2452	2453	2454	2455	2456	2457	2458	2459	2460	2461	2462	2463
9A	2464	2465	2466	2467	2468	2469	2470	2471	2472	2473	2474	2475	2476	2477	2478	2479
9B	2480	2481	2482	2483	2484	2485	2486	2487	2488	2489	2490	2491	2492	2493	2494	2495
9C	2496	2497	2498	2499	2500	2501	2502	2503	2504	2505	2506	2507	2508	2509	2510	2511
9D	2512	2513	2514	2515	2516	2517	2518	2519	2520	2521	2522	2523	2524	2525	2526	2527
9E	2528	2529	2530	2531	2532	2533	2534	2535	2536	2537	2538	2539	2540	2541	2542	2543
9F	2544	2545	2546	2547	2548	2549	2550	2551	2552	2553	2554	2555	2556	2557	2558	2559

HEXADECIMAL-DECIMAL INTEGER CONVERSION (Continued)

	0	1	2	3	4	5	6	7	8	9	A	B	C	D	E	F
A0	2560	2561	2562	2563	2564	2565	2566	2567	2568	2569	2570	2571	2572	2573	2574	2575
A1	2576	2577	2578	2579	2580	2581	2582	2583	2584	2585	2586	2587	2588	2589	2590	2591
A2	2592	2593	2594	2595	2596	2597	2598	2599	2600	2601	2602	2603	2604	2605	2606	2607
A3	2608	2609	2610	2611	2612	2613	2614	2615	2616	2617	2618	2619	2620	2621	2622	2623
A4	2624	2625	2626	2627	2628	2629	2630	2631	2632	2633	2634	2635	2636	2637	2638	2639
A5	2640	2641	2642	2643	2644	2645	2646	2647	2648	2649	2650	2651	2652	2653	2654	2655
A6	2656	2657	2658	2659	2660	2661	2662	2663	2664	2665	2666	2667	2668	2669	2670	2671
A7	2672	2673	2674	2675	2676	2677	2678	2679	2680	2681	2682	2683	2684	2685	2686	2687
A8	2688	2689	2690	2691	2692	2693	2694	2695	2696	2697	2698	2699	2700	2701	2702	2703
A9	2704	2705	2706	2707	2708	2709	2710	2711	2712	2713	2714	2715	2716	2717	2718	2719
AA	2720	2721	2722	2723	2724	2725	2726	2727	2728	2729	2730	2731	2732	2733	2734	2735
AB	2736	2737	2738	2739	2740	2741	2742	2743	2744	2745	2746	2747	2748	2749	2750	2751
AC	2752	2753	2754	2755	2756	2757	2758	2759	2760	2761	2762	2763	2764	2765	2766	2767
AD	2768	2769	2770	2771	2772	2773	2774	2775	2776	2777	2778	2779	2780	2781	2782	2783
AE	2784	2785	2786	2787	2788	2789	2790	2791	2792	2793	2794	2795	2796	2797	2798	2799
AF	2800	2801	2802	2803	2804	2805	2806	2807	2808	2809	2810	2811	2812	2813	2814	2815
B0	2816	2817	2818	2819	2820	2821	2822	2823	2824	2825	2826	2827	2828	2829	2830	2831
B1	2832	2833	2834	2835	2836	2837	2838	2839	2840	2841	2842	2843	2844	2845	2846	2847
B2	2848	2849	2850	2851	2852	2853	2854	2855	2856	2857	2858	2859	2860	2861	2862	2863
B3	2864	2865	2866	2867	2868	2869	2870	2871	2872	2873	2874	2875	2876	2877	2878	2879
B4	2880	2881	2882	2883	2884	2885	2886	2887	2888	2889	2890	2891	2892	2893	2894	2895
B5	2896	2897	2898	2899	2900	2901	2902	2903	2904	2905	2906	2907	2908	2909	2910	2911
B6	2912	2913	2914	2915	2916	2917	2918	2919	2920	2921	2922	2923	2924	2925	2926	2927
B7	2928	2929	2930	2931	2932	2933	2934	2935	2936	2937	2938	2939	2940	2941	2942	2943
B8	2944	2945	2946	2947	2948	2949	2950	2951	2952	2953	2954	2955	2956	2957	2958	2959
B9	2960	2961	2962	2963	2964	2965	2966	2967	2968	2969	2970	2971	2972	2973	2974	2975
BA	2976	2977	2978	2979	2980	2981	2982	2983	2984	2985	2986	2987	2988	2989	2990	2991
BB	2992	2993	2994	2995	2996	2997	2998	2999	3000	3001	3002	3003	3004	3005	3006	3007
BC	3008	3009	3010	3011	3012	3013	3014	3015	3016	3017	3018	3019	3020	3021	3022	3023
BD	3024	3025	3026	3027	3028	3029	3030	3031	3032	3033	3034	3035	3036	3037	3038	3039
BE	3040	3041	3042	3043	3044	3045	3046	3047	3048	3049	3050	3051	3052	3053	3054	3055
BF	3056	3057	3058	3059	3060	3061	3062	3063	3064	3065	3066	3067	3068	3069	3070	3071
C0	3072	3073	3074	3075	3076	3077	3078	3079	3080	3081	3082	3083	3084	3085	3086	3087
C1	3088	3089	3090	3091	3092	3093	3094	3095	3096	3097	3098	3099	3100	3101	3102	3103
C2	3104	3105	3106	3107	3108	3109	3110	3111	3112	3113	3114	3115	3116	3117	3118	3119
C3	3120	3121	3122	3123	3124	3125	3126	3127	3128	3129	3130	3131	3132	3133	3134	3135
C4	3136	3137	3138	3139	3140	3141	3142	3143	3144	3145	3146	3147	3148	3149	3150	3151
C5	3152	3153	3154	3155	3156	3157	3158	3159	3160	3161	3162	3163	3164	3165	3166	3167
C6	3168	3169	3170	3171	3172	3173	3174	3175	3176	3177	3178	3179	3180	3181	3182	3183
C7	3184	3185	3186	3187	3188	3189	3190	3191	3192	3193	3194	3195	3196	3197	3198	3199
C8	3200	3201	3202	3203	3204	3205	3206	3207	3208	3209	3210	3211	3212	3213	3214	3215
C9	3216	3217	3218	3219	3220	3221	3222	3223	3224	3225	3226	3227	3228	3229	3230	3231
CA	3232	3233	3234	3235	3236	3237	3238	3239	3240	3241	3242	3243	3244	3245	3246	3247
CB	3248	3249	3250	3251	3252	3253	3254	3255	3256	3257	3258	3259	3260	3261	3262	3263
CC	3264	3265	3266	3267	3268	3269	3270	3271	3272	3273	3274	3275	3276	3277	3278	3279
CD	3280	3281	3282	3283	3284	3285	3286	3287	3288	3289	3290	3291	3292	3293	3294	3295
CE	3296	3297	3298	3299	3300	3301	3302	3303	3304	3305	3306	3307	3308	3309	3310	3311
CF	3312	3313	3314	3315	3316	3317	3318	3319	3320	3321	3322	3323	3324	3325	3326	3327

HEXADECIMAL-DECIMAL INTEGER CONVERSION (Continued)

	0	1	2	3	4	5	6	7	8	9	A	B	C	D	E	F
D0	3328	3329	3330	3331	3332	3333	3334	3335	3336	3337	3338	3339	3340	3341	3342	3343
D1	3344	3345	3346	3347	3348	3349	3350	3351	3352	3353	3354	3355	3356	3357	3358	3359
D2	3360	3361	3362	3363	3364	3365	3366	3367	3368	3369	3370	3371	3372	3373	3374	3375
D3	3376	3377	3378	3379	3380	3381	3382	3383	3384	3385	3386	3387	3388	3389	3390	3391
D4	3392	3393	3394	3395	3396	3397	3398	3399	3400	3401	3402	3403	3404	3405	3406	3407
D5	3408	3409	3410	3411	3412	3413	3414	3415	3416	3417	3418	3419	3420	3421	3422	3423
D6	3424	3425	3426	3427	3428	3429	3430	3431	3432	3433	3434	3435	3436	3437	3438	3439
D7	3440	3441	3442	3443	3444	3445	3446	3447	3448	3449	3450	3451	3452	3453	3454	3455
D8	3456	3457	3458	3459	3460	3461	3462	3463	3464	3465	3466	3467	3468	3469	3470	3471
D9	3472	3473	3474	3475	3476	3477	3478	3479	3480	3481	3482	3483	3484	3485	3486	3487
DA	3488	3489	3490	3491	3492	3493	3494	3495	3496	3497	3498	3499	3500	3501	3502	3503
DB	3504	3505	3506	3507	3508	3509	3510	3511	3512	3513	3514	3515	3516	3517	3518	3519
DC	3520	3521	3522	3523	3524	3525	3526	3527	3528	3529	3530	3531	3532	3533	3534	3535
DD	3536	3537	3538	3539	3540	3541	3542	3543	3544	3545	3546	3547	3548	3549	3550	3551
DE	3552	3553	3554	3555	3556	3557	3558	3559	3560	3561	3562	3563	3564	3565	3566	3567
DF	3568	3569	3570	3571	3572	3573	3574	3575	3576	3577	3578	3579	3580	3581	3582	3583
E0	3584	3585	3586	3587	3588	3589	3590	3591	3592	3593	3594	3595	3596	3597	3598	3599
E1	3600	3601	3602	3603	3604	3605	3606	3607	3608	3609	3610	3611	3612	3613	3614	3615
E2	3616	3617	3618	3619	3620	3621	3622	3623	3624	3625	3626	3627	3628	3629	3630	3631
E3	3632	3633	3634	3635	3636	3637	3638	3639	3640	3641	3642	3643	3644	3645	3646	3647
E4	3648	3649	3650	3651	3652	3653	3654	3655	3656	3657	3658	3659	3660	3661	3662	3663
E5	3664	3665	3666	3667	3668	3669	3670	3671	3672	3673	3674	3675	3676	3677	3678	3679
E6	3680	3681	3682	3683	3684	3685	3686	3687	3688	3689	3690	3691	3692	3693	3694	3695
E7	3696	3697	3698	3699	3700	3701	3702	3703	3704	3705	3706	3707	3708	3709	3710	3711
E8	3712	3713	3714	3715	3716	3717	3718	3719	3720	3721	3722	3723	3724	3725	3726	3727
E9	3728	3729	3730	3731	3732	3733	3734	3735	3736	3737	3738	3739	3740	3741	3742	3743
EA	3744	3745	3746	3747	3748	3749	3750	3751	3752	3753	3754	3755	3756	3757	3758	3759
EB	3760	3761	3762	3763	3764	3765	3766	3767	3768	3769	3770	3771	3772	3773	3774	3775
EC	3776	3777	3778	3779	3780	3781	3782	3783	3784	3785	3786	3787	3788	3789	3790	3791
ED	3792	3793	3794	3795	3796	3797	3798	3799	3800	3801	3802	3803	3804	3805	3806	3807
EE	3808	3809	3810	3811	3812	3813	3814	3815	3816	3817	3818	3819	3820	3821	3822	3823
EF	3824	3825	3826	3827	3828	3829	3830	3831	3832	3833	3834	3835	3836	3837	3838	3839
F0	3840	3841	3842	3843	3844	3845	3846	3847	3848	3849	3850	3851	3852	3853	3854	3855
F1	3856	3857	3858	3859	3860	3861	3862	3863	3864	3865	3866	3867	3868	3869	3870	3871
F2	3872	3873	3874	3875	3876	3877	3878	3879	3880	3881	3882	3883	3884	3885	3886	3887
F3	3888	3889	3890	3891	3892	3893	3894	3895	3896	3897	3898	3899	3900	3901	3902	3903
F4	3904	3905	3906	3907	3908	3909	3910	3911	3912	3913	3914	3915	3916	3917	3918	3919
F5	3920	3921	3922	3923	3924	3925	3926	3927	3928	3929	3930	3931	3932	3933	3934	3935
F6	3936	3937	3938	3939	3940	3941	3942	3943	3944	3945	3946	3947	3948	3949	3950	3951
F7	3952	3953	3954	3955	3956	3957	3958	3959	3960	3961	3962	3963	3964	3965	3966	3967
F8	3968	3969	3970	3971	3972	3973	3974	3975	3976	3977	3978	3979	3980	3981	3982	3983
F9	3984	3985	3986	3987	3988	3989	3990	3991	3992	3993	3994	3995	3996	3997	3998	3999
FA	4000	4001	4002	4003	4004	4005	4006	4007	4008	4009	4010	4011	4012	4013	4014	4015
FB	4016	4017	4018	4019	4020	4021	4022	4023	4024	4025	4026	4027	4028	4029	4030	4031
FC	4032	4033	4034	4035	4036	4037	4038	4039	4040	4041	4042	4043	4044	4045	4046	4047
FD	4048	4049	4050	4051	4052	4053	4054	4055	4056	4057	4058	4059	4060	4061	4062	4063
FE	4064	4065	4066	4067	4068	4069	4070	4071	4072	4073	4074	4075	4076	4077	4078	4079
FF	4080	4081	4082	4083	4084	4085	4086	4087	4088	4089	4090	4091	4092	4093	4094	4095

C
CBASIC Key Words

ABS	DELETE	INT	OUT	SQR
AND	DIM	INT%	PEEK	STEP
AS	ELSE	LE	POKE	STOP
ASC	END	LEFT$	POS	STR$
ATN	EQ	LEN	PRINT	SUB
BUFF	EXP	LET	RANDOMIZE	TAB
CALL	FEND	LINE	READ	TAN
CHAIN	FILE	LOCAL	RECL	THEN
CHR$	FOR	LOG	RECS	TO
CLOSE	FRE	LPRINTER	REM	UCASE$
COMMAND$	GE	LT	REMARK	USING
COMMON	GO	MATCH	RENAME	VAL
CONCHAR%	GOSUB	MID$	RESTORE	WEND
CONSOLE	GOTO	NE	RETURN	WHILE
CONSTAT%	GT	NEXT	RIGHT$	WIDTH
COS	IF	NOT	RND	XOR
CREATE	INITIALIZE	ON	SGN	
DATA	INP	OPEN	SIN	
DEF	INPUT	OR	SIZE	

Index

Other OSBORNE/McGraw-Hill Publications